STARTING DRAMA

ERIC BOAGEY

Bell & Hyman

Published by
BELL & HYMAN LIMITED
Denmark House
37-39 Queen Elizabeth Street
London SE1 2QB

British Library Cataloguing in Publication Data

Boagey, Eric
Starting drama.
1. College and school drama
I. Title
808.2 PN3175

ISBN 0-7135-2681-5

Designed and edited by Impression

Typeset by Typecast, East Peckham, Kent

Printed in Great Britain by Scotprint Ltd., Musselburgh

Acknowledgements
The author and publishers wish to thank the following for
permission to reproduce photographs:
pp. 4, 5, 6, 8-9, 10, 17, 23, 26, 29 (Jonson), 32, 34, 35, 42,
43, 45, 53 (Kean and Grimaldi) The Mary Evans Picture
Library; pp. 6-7, 14-15 Nobby Clark; pp. 7, 19, 20, 29
(tavern brawl and Shakespeare), 31, 53 (Master Betty) The
Mansell Collection; p. 13 Lauros-Giraudon from the Musée
Condé; pp. 24-25, 57, 58, 60-61, 65, 68, 70 BBC Hulton
Picture Library; pp. 27, 52 (poster and Marie Lloyd), 55
by courtesy of the Trustees of The Victoria and Albert
Museum; pp. 36, 37, 48, 74, 77, 96 Zoë Dominic; pp. 47,
53 (Irving) Richard Southern Collection and Drama
Department Collection in the University of Bristol; p. 62
The National Theatre; p. 73 Donald Cooper; p. 84 Etienne
Bertrand Weill.

They would also like to thank the following for permission
to reproduce extracts from plays:
pp. 9-10 'King Oedipus' by Sophocles in *The Theban Plays*
(Penguin); pp. 15-17 'Noah's Flood' in *Everyman and
Medieval Miracle Plays* by A C Cawley (ed) (Dent);
pp. 17-18 *The Cagebirds* by David Campton (Samuel
French); p. 25 'Countdown' by Alan Ayckbourn in *Mixed
Doubles* (Samuel French); p. 40 review of *She Stoops to
Conquer* by Milton Shulman in the *Evening Standard*;
p. 44 'The Vampire or The Bride of the Isles' in *The Golden
Age of Melodrama* (Wolf); pp. 59-61 *Saint Joan* by Bernard
Shaw (Longman); pp. 68-69 *Look Back in Anger* by John
Osborne (Faber); pp. 72-75 *Sergeant Musgrave's Dance*
by John Arden (Methuen); p. 76 *Night School* by Harold
Pinter (Eyre Methuen); p. 77 *Silence* by Harold Pinter (Eyre
Methuen); and the diagram on p. 81 from 'Theatre Staff'
by Clive Barker in *Effective Theatre* by J R Brown
(Heinemann).

CONTENTS

PART 1 – DRAMA THROUGH THE AGES

The Greek Theatre 4
The Medieval Theatre 12
The Elizabethan Theatre 20
The Restoration and After 31
The Nineteenth Century 42
The Twentieth Century 1900-1950 55
The Twentieth Century 1950 to the present 67

PART 2 – BEHIND THE SCENES

Introductory Exercises 82
Voices 84
Mime 85
Acting 85
Exercises in the Basic Skills 88
Improvisation 90
Make-up 93
Stage Design 95

PRESENTER 1

It was in Ancient Greece that the first theatre of Western civilisation began. It flourished in the 5th and 4th centuries BC and produced some of the finest plays the world knows, many of which are still performed today.

PRESENTER 2

The drama had its roots in religious ritual and celebration, particularly in the worship of Dionysus, the god of festivity. Starting in village festivals, the ceremony moved to the cities, where it became one of the great occasions of the Greek year. It was called the City Dionysia and almost all the people of Athens would attend to witness performances of plays that had been chosen by competition.

Nikos was a boy in Athens at that time and this is how he remembers the City Dionysia:

NIKOS

It was April and the festival had begun. There was a magnificent procession on the first day in which all the performers took part. Very solemnly the statue of Dionysus was carried from his temple towards the Academy. It was returned later that night in a torchlit procession and placed in the centre of the great theatre on the hillside where we later watched the plays. Everything was festive – an odd mixture of the serious and the comic. The sacrificing of the goat, the dancing, flute-playing and the chanting of hymns were all the run-up to the festival of plays.

The plays started in the early morning, so we began our walk up the hillside at dawn. As we took our seats in the amphitheatre, I looked down on the circle in which the plays were performed. It was like being one of the gods to be so high! I imagined the actors getting ready behind the stage building – trying on their masks, putting on their heavy gowns, waiting for the moment of silence before they began. The Chorus were there too. When they spoke it was as if only one person spoke. They had long training, of course, not only in their speaking, but in singing and dancing too.

My father had heard that the plays that year were of a very high quality. On each of the three days there were three tragedies and one comedy. I much preferred the comedy to the tragedies. The actors made us laugh and it was a relief to be able to laugh after watching one tragedy after another. My father said I shouldn't expect to be amused at the festival. He said it was a serious religious occasion and I suppose he was right. The plays told us the stories of our heroes and gods and showed how good and evil are always in conflict. There were performances of plays by Sophocles which told the story of King Oedipus. We were told the story in school, so I knew what would happen. It still sent shivers down my spine!

On the last day there was the prizegiving. I liked that. My father said Sophocles would win the ivy-wreath for the best dramatist – as usual he was right!

PRESENTER 1

The drama competition was held every year. Dramatists were asked to submit four plays in

Greek actors' masks

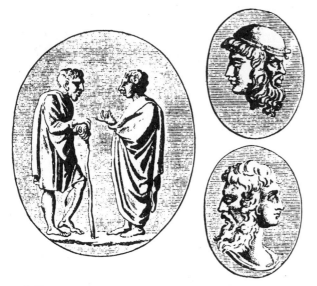

all. Three had to be tragedies and one a comedy. Judges were appointed to choose the three best dramatists and these would have their plays performed in the festival on three separate days. Each dramatist was given a leading actor to perform the main part in the play and, even more important, a wealthy man of Athens who, as part of his civic duty, would pay all the expenses of the production.

PRESENTER 2
On the third day of the festival there was the classical equivalent of the Oscar ceremony, when the prizes were awarded for the best tragedy, the best comedy, the best production and the best actor. To be crowned with an ivy-wreath for writing the best tragedy was considered one of the greatest honours an Athenian citizen could receive.

PRESENTER 1
The **Chorus** was originally a group of 50 speakers who recited the story in verse with a leader. Drama itself really started when an actor named **Thespis** had the idea of one person breaking away from the Chorus and speaking independently — in fact, replying to what the Chorus said. Eventually the number in the Chorus was reduced to 12, but increased again to 15 by the dramatist whom Nikos's father thought would win the competition — Sophocles. As the Chorus got smaller, the number of actors increased, but only to three!

PRESENTER 2
Eventually the Chorus lost its importance and became merely a small group of singers and dancers who were used to break up the action of the play with short interludes.

PRESENTER 1
You might ask how a drama could be presented successfully with no more than three actors, particularly the Greek drama with its powerful stories from myth and legend. Part of the answer was that there were performers who did not speak (and weren't considered 'actors'), but who represented people in the play. More important, however, was the use of masks, which enabled one actor to play several parts by simply putting on a different mask.

PRESENTER 2
Masks were made of wood with linen stretched over them. They fitted completely over the face, but had large open mouths which helped to magnify the sound of the voice. There were over 30 masks commonly in use. They represented not only a type of character, such as young, old, rich and poor, but also the emotions that were typical of the character, like rage, fear, hate and despair. What expressions do you think the comic masks would represent?

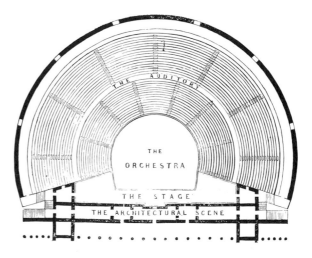

PRESENTER 1
Just as the masks helped the audience to recognise the characters easily, so the costumes of the actors were intended to show the characters on a larger-than-life scale. The actors wore striking robes of bright colours, adorned with heavy embroidery. However, the style of costume had a special meaning for the audience: purple robes indicated the

5

characters were royalty; a short leather tunic would be worn by a shepherd; long, trailing robes implied grief; and if a character wore a hat it meant he was going on a journey.

PRESENTER 2

In order to increase their height the actors wore high boots with thick platform soles, and tall, elaborate headdresses. These costumes and accessories helped to make the actors appear more imposing and dignified.

PRESENTER 1

The Chorus, however, wore the dress of the people they represented and much lighter masks than the actors. The comic characters in the less serious plays usually wore soft slippers, flesh-coloured tights and a short tunic.

PRESENTER 2

The theatres themselves were vast, yet the thousands of people in the audience could hear every word the actors said – the acoustics were so perfect.

PRESENTER 1

Some of the classical theatres remain to this day and are still used. In 1982 the National Theatre's production of *The Oresteia* by Aeschylus, in which all the actors wore masks, was performed at the theatre in Epidaurus to great critical acclaim. So we can hardly say that the Greek theatre is a thing of the past, can we?

Ten QUICK QUESTIONS

1 In what season was the City Dionysia held?
2 At what time of day did performances of the plays begin?
3 How many plays were performed on a single day?
4 What were the responsibilities of the wealthy man who sponsored the plays?
5 How did the Chorus change over the years?
6 Why were the masks important in the performance of the plays?
7 Describe a typical mask.
8 Give two examples of the way in which costume could tell the audience something about the characters.
9 In what ways did the actors make themselves look 'larger than life'?
10 What prizes were awarded at the end of the drama festival?

FINDING OUT FOR YOURSELF

Use dictionaries and encyclopedias to help you answer the following questions.

- Many of the words we use in the theatre today have their origin in Greek words. Look up the meaning of these words and, if possible, find out which Greek words they come from:
  amphitheatre protagonist proscenium tragedy chorus comedy thespian

- Can you find out more about **Dionysus** and **Thespis**?

- Nikos mentioned the dramatist **Sophocles**. He was one of several famous Greek dramatists whose works have survived from the classical period. Find out what you can about these writers:
  Aeschylus Sophocles Euripides Aristophanes
  For instance, you could find out when they lived, what kinds of play they wrote, what stories they told in their plays, how they changed the Greek theatre, and how many times each won a prize.

WRITING ABOUT THE GREEK THEATRE

1 Imagine that you are staying with Nikos during the City Dionysia. Write an account of what you did and saw, starting with the procession of the statue and going on to a description of the performance in the amphitheatre. Use the information you have been given in this chapter, including the diagrams and illustrations.

2 Do you think you would have enjoyed a day at the Greek theatre? How would it have contrasted with a theatre visit today?

3 The remains of several Greek amphitheatres are visited by tourists every year. You are a courier or guide, conducting a group of tourists over one of the Greek amphitheatres in the heat of summer. Write out the commentary for your guided tour.

Theatre at Epidaurus
TOP LEFT National Theatre production of the *Oresteia*

SOPHOCLES

Sophocles was born at Colonus, near Athens, in 496 BC and was 90 when he died. He wrote over 100 plays and of these at least 24 won first prize in the festival competitions. Only seven of his plays survive and the greatest of these are usually considered to be the three depicting the life and fortunes of Oedipus: *King Oedipus*, *Antigone* and *Oedipus at Colonus*.

THE LEGEND OF OEDIPUS

A son was born to LAIUS, King of Thebes, and his wife, JOCASTA, but the rejoicing was overcast by a prophecy of the oracle that the child was fated to kill his father and marry his mother. To prevent this prophecy coming true, Laius ordered a servant to abandon the child on a mountainside and to pierce its feet with an iron pin to prevent it crawling away. The servant, however, took pity on the child and gave it to a shepherd to look after. The shepherd took it to his master, the King of Corinth, who, being childless, decided to adopt it and bring it up as his own son. He named the child OEDIPUS, or 'Swollen-foot'.

Oedipus grew to manhood assuming the King and Queen to be his real parents, but by chance he learnt of the prophecy that he would be the slayer of his father and, to prevent this happening, he fled from Corinth. During his travels he quarrelled with a man in a horse-drawn carriage and in the struggle he killed him. Without realising it, Oedipus had killed his real father, Laius.

Oedipus made his way to Thebes and found the city in the grip of a monster – the Sphinx. By finding the answer to the riddle the Sphinx posed, Oedipus freed the city and was rewarded by being made king. He married Jocasta, the widow of Laius, and she bore him four children. Fifteen years of prosperity went by, but the gods could not let the truth be concealed for ever. Pestilence and famine returned to Thebes and their cause was gradually traced to Oedipus himself, who was revealed as both the son and the killer of Laius. Jocasta, unable to bear the shame of her marriage, hanged herself; and Oedipus, on seeing her body, pierced his eyes with her golden brooches and blinded himself.

WHERE THREE ROADS MEET | An extract from *King Oedipus*

The following extract is taken from *King Oedipus*. Oedipus has just quarrelled violently with CREON, Jocasta's brother, whom he accuses of plotting against the throne and slandering him as being the murderer of Laius.

JOCASTA	Will you not tell me too? Tell me, I implore you,
	Why you have conceived this terrible hatred against him.
OEDIPUS	I will. You are more to me than these good men.
	The fault is Creon's, and his this plot against me.
JOCASTA	How was it his? What is the accusation?
OEDIPUS	He says the murder of Laius was my doing.
JOCASTA	From his own knowledge, or other men's report?
OEDIPUS	Ah, there's his cleverness; he shields himself
	By using a rascally soothsayer as his tool.
JOCASTA	Then absolve yourself at once. For I can tell you,
	No man possesses the secret of divination.
	And I have proof. An oracle was given to Laius –
	From Phoebus, no; but from his ministers –
	That he should die by the hands of his own child,
	His child and mine. What came of it? Laius,
	It is common knowledge, was killed by outland robbers
	At a place where three roads meet. As for the child,
	It was not yet three days old, when he cast it out
	(By other hands, not his) with rivetted ankles
	To perish on the empty mountain-side.
	There, then, Apollo did not so contrive it.
	The offspring did not kill the father; the father,
	For all his fears, was killed – not by his son.
	Yet such were the prophets' warnings. Why should you,
	Then, heed them for a moment? What he intends,
	The god will show us in his own good time.
OEDIPUS	My wife, what you have said has troubled me.
	My mind goes back ... and something in me moves ...
JOCASTA	Why? What is the matter? How you turn and start!
OEDIPUS	Did you not say that Laius was killed
	At a place where three roads meet?
JOCASTA	That was the story;
	And is the story still.
OEDIPUS	Where? In what country?
JOCASTA	The land called Phocis – where the road divides,
	Leading to Delphi and to Daulia.
OEDIPUS	How long ago did it happen?
JOCASTA	It became known
	A little time before your reign began.
OEDIPUS	O God, what wilt thou do to me!

JOCASTA	Why, Oedipus, What weighs upon your mind?
OEDIPUS	O do not ask! But tell me, what was Laius like? How old?
JOCASTA	Tall – silver-frosted hair – about your figure.
OEDIPUS	Ah, wretch! Am I unwittingly self-cursed?
JOCASTA	What, O my King, what is it? You frighten me.
OEDIPUS	Had then the prophet eyes? O is it possible? To prove it certain, tell me one thing more.
JOCASTA	You frighten me. I will tell you all I know.
OEDIPUS	How was the King attended? By a few, Or in full state with numerous bodyguard?
JOCASTA	Five men in all, a herald leading them; One carriage only, in which King Laius rode.
OEDIPUS	Clearer, alas, too clear! Who told you this?
JOCASTA	A servant, the only survivor that returned.
OEDIPUS	Is he still in the household?
JOCASTA	No. When he came back, And found you king in his late master's place, He earnestly begged me to let him go away Into the country to become a shepherd, Far from the city's eyes. I let him go. Poor fellow, he might have asked a greater favour; He was a good slave.
OEDIPUS	Could we have him here Without delay?
JOCASTA	We could. Why do you ask?
OEDIPUS	O wife, I fear … I fear that I have said Too much, and therefore I must see this man.
JOCASTA	Well you shall see him. Meantime, may I not hear What weighs so heavily on your heart?

DISCUSSION POINTS

Why is it possible to enjoy seeing the same play twice?

The Greek audience would know the story of Oedipus before they saw the play. Do you think the effect of the tragedy would be diminished because of this?

If you were producing a Greek tragedy in a small theatre with a proscenium-arch stage, what would be your approach? What type of stage-set would you use? What style of acting would you go for?

Greek tragedy is sometimes played in modern dress. If you were to update the situation in the Oedipus extract, what changes would you make? How would you dress the play? How would you deal with the Chorus?

ACTING

1 In the extract from *King Oedipus* the questions are used to draw out information in sharp, quickly-moving dialogue. Try introducing this technique into your own play by creating a situation in which one character seeks information from another and in doing so gradually reveals the details of a past happening.

You will have to decide *where* the scene takes place, *who* the characters are, and *what* has happened. Here are some suggestions:

WHERE	WHO	WHAT
a hideout	a waiting mother	a fight
a camp	a returned son/daughter	an accident
a kitchen	a passer-by	a theft
a hospital	a victim	a discovery
a police station	husband and wife	a confession
an airport lounge	policeman	an ordeal
a room	soldier	a raid

Discuss the development of the play, improvise the scenes and, if you wish, produce a script.

2 Oedipus begins by being offended at the accusations levelled against him, but ends feeling horrified at the possibility that he might be guilty. You will find some ideas for improvisations on this theme under the heading 'Changing the Emotion' on page 91.

11

The Medieval Theatre

THE FIRST PLAYS

PRESENTER 1
Drama in England began in the church.

PRESENTER 2
The first play was four lines long and it contained four characters. It was written in Latin and it was inserted into the regular Easter service.

PRESENTER 1
Imagine that we are members of the congregation, sitting in our pews in church. We are looking towards the altar, which we have to imagine is the tomb of Christ. A priest is standing by the altar. He represents the angel guarding the tomb. Towards him walk three other priests, representing the three Marys. Translated into English, this is what they say:

ANGEL	Whom do you seek at the sepulchre, O Christian women?
MARYS	Jesus of Nazareth, who was crucified, O heavenly one.
ANGEL	He is not here. He has risen even as he foretold. Go: proclaim that he has risen from the sepulchre.

PRESENTER 2
From this small beginning drama developed.

PRESENTER 1
At first, the church itself was the 'theatre' and the plays became known as **Liturgical Plays** because they formed part of the liturgy, or church service.

PRESENTER 2
The plays were performed, not only by the altar, but in the body of the church itself. In the centre of the church – called the 'nave' – little scenes would be constructed. These represented the places associated with the story of Christ – such as Bethlehem, Nazareth, Herod's Palace, etc. The actors would move from one scene to another and the congregation would stand and watch.

PRESENTER 1
The Liturgical Plays became increasingly popular. The ordinary people loved the entertainment they were getting in church! The plays became longer, more characters were added, they were presented more often throughout the year, but . . .

PRESENTER 2
. . . the clergy were less happy. The churches often couldn't hold the crowds of people who turned up. The strictly religious content of the church service was beginning to take second place to the plays themselves, particularly when the Latin began to give way to English dialogue.

PRESENTER 1
The church authorities decided to act. The plays would no longer be performed inside the church, but outside in the surrounding grounds.

PRESENTER 2
And they would no longer be part of the regular church service, but independent performances.

PRESENTER 1
Moreover, the priests were told by the church authorities that they must no longer act in the plays.

PRESENTER 2

The way was open for the townspeople to take over and the creation of the most remarkable dramas of the medieval period began – the **Mystery Plays**.

PRESENTER 1

No, they weren't medieval whodunits! The word 'mystery' meant trade or craft, and the plays were performed by members of the craft guilds during Holy Week. They dramatised stories of the Bible from the Creation, through the Nativity and Resurrection to the Last Judgment. The cities of York, Chester and Wakefield produced complete sets of these plays, which were called 'cycles'.

PRESENTER 2

Each guild presented one play from the cycle. The play usually had some connection with the craft of the guild itself.

PRESENTER 1

The shipwrights would present *The Building of the Ark*, the fishermen and fishmongers would do *Noah and the Flood*, the nail-makers *The Crucifixion* and the bakers *The Last Supper*. Every play had to be given official approval and the standard demanded was extremely high.

PRESENTER 2

And though the actors were all amateur, they did receive some payment from the guilds. We still have some records of these payments:

PRESENTER 1

. . . for cock-crowing – fourpence
to Robert Brown playing God – sixpence
for hanging Judas – fourpence . . .

PRESENTER 2

The plays were performed on pageant-wagons, which would be pulled from one location in the town to another. As one wagon moved away, another took its place, till the cycle was completed.

PRESENTER 1

The guildsmen worked hard, rehearsing, making costumes and masks, designing scenery and special effects. The actors had to be ready in their pageants at 5 a.m. on the days of the performance and were fined six shillings and eightpence if they were late. One young man who couldn't risk being late was Stephen Wagstaffe. He played Adam.

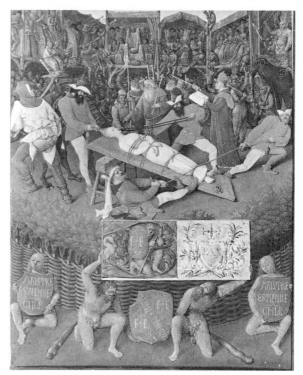

A wicker stage used in France *c.* 1460

STEPHEN

Of course, I was glad when our play was chosen, though I was a bit worried when the Master of my Guild, the Tanners, told me I was to play Adam, for I thought I would have to appear naked and I couldn't face that. Then they said I was to wear a costume of white leather which would just make me *appear* naked and I felt a lot happier. But I hadn't reckoned on how hot it would be, covered all over in leather. Eve felt the same, though I suppose the Garden of Eden must have been in a hot country if they had snakes there! Well, we met at half past four in the morning, and we changed into our costumes in the lower part of the wagon. Then we towed our wagon to the city gate where we were to give our first performance. We were following *The Fall of Lucifer*, a play that always starts off the play-cycle. At the signal from the gaffer we climbed onto the upper platform and began the first of our 15 performances that day.

PRESENTER 2

The plays were serious, but they were also popular entertainments. Into the Biblical stories

13

the anonymous writers slipped scenes from contemporary medieval life. Comic characters were created, like the villainous Satan, the ranting Herod and Mak the sheep-stealer, all of whom became established favourites with the audience.

PRESENTER 1
Once again the church authorities became anxious. A declaration was issued in York forbidding the performance of plays that 'tended to the maintenance of superstition and idolatry or which were contrary to the laws of God or the Realm'.

PRESENTER 2
What was happening was that what we call 'theatre' was beginning to take shape. The foundations were being laid for a drama that would have its climax in the Elizabethan period.

PRESENTER 1
Yet the Mystery Plays were not to be the only influence on the new drama. There were the **Morality Plays** which, although still religious in intention, concerned themselves with the lives of ordinary people –

PRESENTER 2
– or, more accurately, the vices and virtues of ordinary people. The characters were given names like Greed, Envy, Lust, Truth and Justice.

PRESENTER 1
They were personifications and the plays aimed at teaching people that goodness brings heavenly reward, whilst sin leads to eternal punishment.

PRESENTER 2
The plays were performed out of doors as the Mysteries were, but now the plots were invented by the authors. The performers were no longer guildsmen, but members of local acting associations specially formed for the purpose.

PRESENTER 1
Now we begin to see how the acting profession started. Alongside the amateur companies there were small groups of actors, often including the minstrels who sang in the great houses. These groups performed plays during the festive seasons, like Christmas, before the lord and his guests. During the rest of the year they went on tour. The plays they acted were fairly short, with few characters, and they were called **Interludes**.

PRESENTER 2
So from a simple beginning in church in the 13th century, drama had acquired a stage, properties, make-up, playwrights and professional acting companies. It wasn't such a big step to the opening of the first purpose-built theatre in 1576.

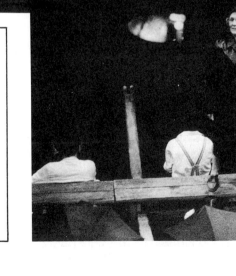

TEN QUICK QUESTIONS

1 What was a 'Liturgical Play'?
2 What was the subject of the first play?
3 Why did performances move out of the church?
4 How did the 'Mystery Plays' get their name?
5 Who acted in them?
6 What was a 'cycle' of plays?
7 Which cities had cycles of Mystery Plays?
8 At what time did performances begin?
9 How did the 'Morality Plays' differ from the Mysteries?
10 How did professional acting develop?

NOAH'S FLOOD | An extract from *The Deluge*

We heard that the Mystery Plays presented the stories of the Bible through typically medieval characters. Here's an example, from *The Deluge*, which was part of the Coventry Cycle. All the animals that are to enter the Ark are painted on boards and correspond to the names in the script. Noah's sons and their wives enter the Ark, but Noah's wife refuses, unless her friends ('GOSSIPS') can go with her.

[*Then* NOAH *shall go into the Ark with all his family, his* WIFE *except, and the Ark must be boarded round about, and on the boards all the beasts and fowls hereafter rehearsed must be painted, that these words may agree with the pictures.*]

Noah's Flood – National Theatre production

SHEM	Sir, here are lions, leopards in, Horses, mares, oxen, and swine; Goats, calves, sheep, and kine Here sitten thou may see.	
HAM	Camels, asses men may find, Buck, doe, hart, and hind; And beasts of all manner kind Here be, as thinketh me.	
JAPHETH	Take here cats and dogs too, Otter, fox, fulmart also; Hares hopping gaily can go Have cole here for to eat.	*polecat* *cabbage*
NOAH'S WIFE	And here are bears, wolves set; Apes, owls, marmoset, Weasels, squirrels, and ferret; Here they eat their meat.	*lying*
SHEM'S WIFE	Yet more beasts are in this house: Here cats maken it full crouse; Here a ratton, here a mouse, They stand nigh together.	*rat*
HAM'S WIFE	And here are fowls, less and more: Herons, cranes, and bittor, Swans, peacocks; and them before Meat for this weather.	*small and big* *bittern*
JAPHETH'S WIFE	Here are cocks, kites, crows, Rooks, ravens, many rows, Ducks, curlews, whoever knows Each one in his kind; And here are doves, digs, drakes, Redshanks running through the lakes; And each fowl that leden makes In this ship men may find.	*ducks* *song*
NOAH	Wife, come in! Why stands thou there? Thou art ever froward, that dare I swear. Come in, on God's half! Time it were, For fear lest that we drown.	*perverse*

NOAH'S WIFE	Yea, sir, set up your sail,	
	And row forth with evil hail,	
	For, without any fail,	*doubt*
	I will not out of this town.	
	But I have my gossips every one,	*unless;*
	One foot further I will not gone;	*go*
	They shall not drown, by St John,	
	And I may save their life.	*if*
	They loved me full well, by Christ;	
	But thou wilt let them in thy chest,	*ark*
	Else row forth, Noah, whither thou list,	*wish*
	And get thee a new wife.	
NOAH	Shem, son, lo! thy mother is wrow:	*angry*
	Forsooth, such another I do not know.	
SHEM	Father, I shall fetch her in, I trow,	*swear*
	Without any fail [*He goes to his mother.*]	
	Mother, my father after thee sent,	
	And bids thee into yonder ship wend.	*go*
	Look up and see the wind,	
	For we be ready to sail.	
NOAH'S WIFE	Son, go again to him, and say	
	I will not come therein to-day.	
NOAH	Come in, wife, in twenty devils way,	
	Or else stand there without.	
HAM	Shall we all fetch her in?	
NOAH	Yea, sons, in Christ's blessing and mine;	*with*
	I would you hied you betime,	*hurried*
	For of this flood I am in doubt.	*afraid*
GOSSIP [TO WIFE]	The flood comes fleeting in full fast,	*flowing*
	On every side it spreads full far;	
	For fear of drowning I am aghast;	
	Good gossip, let us draw near.	
	And let us drink ere we depart,	
	For oft-times we have done so;	
	For at a draught thou drink'st a quart,	
	And so will I do ere I go.	
NOAH'S WIFE	Here is a pottle of Malmsey, good and strong;	
	It will rejoice both heart and tongue;	
	Though Noah thinks us never so long,	
	Yet we will drink alike.	
JAPHETH	Mother, we pray you altogether –	
	For we are here your own childer –	*children*
	Come into the ship for fear of the weather,	
	For his love that you bought!	*redeemed*
NOAH'S WIFE	That will I not, for all your call,	
	But I have my gossips all.	*unless*
SHEM	In faith, mother, yet you shall,	
	Whether you will or nought. [*They carry her into the ark.*]	
NOAH	Welcome, wife, into this boat.	
NOAH'S WIFE	And have thou that for thy note! [*She boxes him on the ear.*]	
NOAH	Aha! marry, this is hot!	
	It is good to be still.	*peaceful*
	Ah, children, methinks my boat removes;	*moves*
	Our tarrying here hugely me grieves.	

Over the land the water spreads;
God do as he will!

Ah, great God that art so good,
That works not thy will is wood.
Now all this world is on a flood,
As I well see in sight.
This window will I shut anon,
And into my chamber will I gone,
Till this water, so great one,
Be slaked through thy might.

whoever; mad

PERSONIFICATIONS

The characters in the Morality Plays were personifications and they were later succeeded by individualised characters; but the technique of using personification in drama has also been used in the 20th century in a play called *The Cagebirds* by David Campton. The characters include the LONG-TONGUED GOSSIP, the MIRROR-EYED GAZER, the MEDICATED GLOOM, the REGULAR THUMP, the CONSTANT TWITTING and the GREAT GUZZLE.

Here is an excerpt. The scene is a room with a single large door. In it are the 'cagebirds', looked after by the MISTRESS.

WHERE ARE MY SWEETIES? | An extract from *The Cagebirds* by David Campton

	[*The* MISTRESS's *voice is heard off. Ideally this would be an amplified whisper.*]
MISTRESS	[*off*] Sweeties. Sweeties, sweeties, sweeties.
	[*The* LADIES *look at each other, then immediately try to appear as though they had not.*]
	[*off*] Where are my sweeties?
	[*The* LADIES *get up and move about rapidly, but aimlessly – talking, but never listening.*]
GUZZLE	Surely it must be tea-time. Where are the muffins and crumpets? Where are the toasted tea-cakes? Where is the thin-cut bread and butter? Where is the tea?
GLOOM	Warm wrapping. That's the only answer. Lagging, if you look at it from the plumber's point of view. Why should we

17

	cosset our pipes, but neglect our torsos? Medicated wool is the answer. Yards of it.
GAZER	I've been experimenting with underwater shades – pearl, coral, and anemone. Youthful tints. Far too youthful to be left to mere youth. Pearl, and coral, and sea something. Has anyone noticed?
GOSSIP	Only one leg. That's a fact. I heard it myself. That makes you think, doesn't it? Someone has some explaining to do if you ask me. All those years and only one leg.
THUMP	The rot must be stopped. That's what a dentist does with a decaying tooth. He stops it. This is a decaying society. It must be stopped before the rot spreads.
TWITTING	This is all so unsettling. Nothing stays the same for more than two seconds running. Even the barometer goes up and down like clockwork. How can one trust in anything when everything is always changing?
	[*Pause. There is the amplified sound of a key being turned in a lock. The* LADIES *move about and talk even faster.*]
GUZZLE	Tea-cakes. Tea-cakes. Tea-cakes. Cream buns and puff-paste. Tea. Tea. Tea.
GLOOM	Warm. Warmer. Warmest. Wrap up. Avoid draughts. Keep warm. Warmer. Warmest.
GAZER	Beautiful for ever. Health and beauty. Home and beauty. Sleep. Beauty. Sleep.
GOSSIP	No. No. Not a word. Listen to this. Did you ever? No, no.
THUMP	Stop. Stop. Stop. Down with it. Out with it. Away with it. Stop. Stop. Stop.
TWITTING	Not again. Oh, not again. This is too much. Much too much. Not again.
	[*The door is opened. Everyone stands very still, very quiet.* *The* MISTRESS *stands in the doorway. She is a smiling and bent but authoritative person, older than the* LADIES, *and, if possible taller than any of them.*]
MISTRESS	Here are my sweeties. [*She shuts the door behind her and advances into the room.*] How are my sweeties?
	[*The* LADIES *move about again, but in turn come up to the* MISTRESS.]
TWITTING	It's the uncertainty that bothers me. If only I could be sure about anything. But I'm not. One day I think one way, and the next day I think the opposite.
MISTRESS	That's because you're a permanently floating voter.
TWITTING	Am I? Am I really? Oh, thank you so much.
THUMP	Sex and violence. You've seen it, haven't you? Even in comics. I've made a study of comics. Lurid with lust and bad jokes. It's a problem.
MISTRESS	But in such safe hands.
THUMP	The censor. That's what we need. Bring back the censor.
GLOOM	Have you been inoculated against rabies?
MISTRESS	Against everything.
GLOOM	How wise.
GOSSIP	Have you heard?
MISTRESS	Whisper.

18

PRACTICAL WORK

1 Take this short extract as an exercise in developing characters based on personifications. In relation to each character, consider: facial expressions; movements; style of speech; costume and make-up.

Learn parts, rehearse the scene and present it before the drama group.

2 When we describe a person's character, we often say things like: 'She's very generous' or 'He's always grumbling' or 'He's a great joker!' What we are doing is to pick out a dominant characteristic, which is another way of looking at personifications.

What features have you found predominating in people you know or in characters in drama and fiction?

When you have discussed this, work on presenting short scenes in which each character has a strong personality feature. Explore what happens when these characters are thrown together in a life situation.

Below are some suggestions for situations and human types, but before working on the scene itself, do some exercises in walking, sitting, talking, facial expressions and movements to get the 'feel' of the character you are going to portray.

an old people's home	enthusiastic
	pessimistic
	stingy
the gang	worrier
	practical type
prison yard	ruthless
	conscientious
survivors	reckless
	cautious
	scared
	I-told-you-so
	blamer
outing	grateful
	optimistic
building site	couldn't-care-less

WRITTEN WORK

1 You are a member of one of the medieval guilds and you are taking part in one of the Mystery Plays. Describe the preparations you made for the play and the performance itself.

2 Write a short play based on a story or incident from the Bible. You can either update the story to the 20th century or, sticking to the original setting, include some modern touches in the characters and dialogue.

3 Write an account of the development of the drama from the first ecclesiastical play to the performance of Interludes.

The Elizabethan Theatre

PRESENTER 1
The travelling actors of the 16th century – descendants of the medieval players of Interludes – used to give performances in the yards of inns throughout the country. The inns provided a ready-made audience of travellers and convenient balconies from which to watch the play. A collection followed and the actors shared their profits with the landlord.

PRESENTER 2
However, the city authorities were unhappy with what was going on. They claimed that there was a danger of spreading the plague from the gathering together of people to watch plays. Also, being rather puritan, they had a deep-seated objection to all forms of entertainment and particularly to the presentation of plays, which they thought encouraged immorality.

PRESENTER 1
They created so many difficulties that eventually the professional actors felt that the only alternative was to establish a theatre of their own outside the city boundaries so that the authorities could have no jurisdiction over them.

PRESENTER 2
In 1576, therefore, the first specially-built theatre in this country came into existence in Finsbury Fields. It was called simply **The Theatre** and it was built by James Burbage.

PRESENTER 1
The Theatre was a great success, both artistically and commercially, for James Burbage had the brilliant idea of making the audience pay to enter the building before they had even seen the play.

PRESENTER 2
Soon new theatres were springing up elsewhere in London – all outside the city boundaries – and particularly on the South Bank of the Thames . . .

PRESENTER 1
. . . The Curtain in 1577, The Rose in 1587, The Swan in 1595 and – most famous of all – The Globe in 1598. It was in The Globe that many of Shakespeare's plays were first performed.

PRESENTER 2
It was owned by a company of actors called The Lord Chamberlain's Men, who included Shakespeare and Richard Burbage, the actor son of James. It was the most successful of all the acting companies and performed plays at royal residences before Queen Elizabeth and her successor, James I. Indeed, James eventually adopted it as his own company and gave it the title 'The King's Men'.

PRESENTER 1
To this small, octagonal building with its centre open to the skies, Londoners came flocking to see the latest plays – amongst them a young tailor's apprentice named Peter.

PETER
Sometimes my master let me have an afternoon off to go to the theatre and I prayed that the

weather would be fine and the performance go forward. When I'd crossed London Bridge I looked for the little flag flying on top of The Globe to signify all was well, but I muttered curses to myself if I heard the trumpet as well, for that told me that the play was about to begin and I would be too late to get a good place in front of the stage. I liked to get there early, pay my penny to the gatherer at the door and find myself a good place in the yard, just in front of the stage. I'd be standing for two or three hours and I didn't want to get stuck in the middle of the crowd behind an oaf with a big head. Sometimes I paid the penny extra and went into the gallery and *sat* through the performance – a real luxury! There were nearly 3000 people in the audience when I saw *Romeo and Juliet* – 3000! That's a lot of pennies – and a lot of noise and hustle and bustle, not to mention flirting with the girls. Not everyone went to see the play!

PRESENTER 2
Peter would be called a 'groundling' because he stood, with hundreds of others, on the ground surrounding the stage, but there were other members of the audience of a higher social class who actually sat on the stage throughout the performance. One of them was called Le Beau.

LE BEAU
Going to the theatre isn't about seeing a play at all, it's about dressing up and being admired! Sitting on the stage, as one does, one is the centre of attraction – and it's very pleasant, even if the groundlings in the yard do hiss and boo us as we walk in! The curs! It's their spitting I can't bear, especially when the wretched stuff goes on my doublet! But the plays can be *so* tedious at times. Those long speeches and the pathetic little band of boy-players who have to represent an army! One can chat to one's friend during the dull passages, but occasionally there is simply nothing for it but to walk out!

PRESENTER 1
We have to remember that in the Elizabethan period, plays had very few performances – unlike today when a popular play can run for years in the West End.

PRESENTER 2
We have a record of The Lord Admiral's Men – a rival company to Shakespeare's. In a period of four weeks in the late autumn of 1595 they put on no fewer than 15 different plays, 10 of which were given only one performance.

PRESENTER 1
In those days, however, plays were not rehearsed and directed as they are now. The Elizabethan actor would learn his lines and his cues, but he wouldn't analyse his part as a modern actor does. He might not even have a complete script – for scripts were expensive to copy and there was a danger of them being stolen by rival companies – but only his part written out. The play had to come together in performance.

PRESENTER 2
And because the average acting company consisted of about 15 actors, there was a lot of doubling-up. The 'stars', like Richard Burbage, who played the great tragic roles in Shakespeare's plays, were the exceptions. The lesser members of the company, particularly the boy-actors, would probably play several roles. Here's Dickie, one of the boys from The Lord Chamberlain's Men.

DICKIE
I'm an apprentice actor and I am learning the craft from one of the older actors in our company. I learnt the trick of crying the other day – real tears! I held an onion in my handkerchief and sniffed hard! I wept tears galore!

We usually get small parts, sometimes several in one play. We might be soldiers in the army, attendant lords, fairies, children, but we excel in the female roles. Women do not act on our stage – it is considered unseemly – and you will find that there are few female characters in Elizabethan plays. But in each company there are usually two or three boys who are well fitted for the female parts, even great characters like Portia, Rosalind, Juliet and Cleopatra in Will Shakespeare's plays. He often made his heroines disguise themselves as boys and so the boys playing the parts become even more convincing. The boys are highly respected for their talent and the audience is not in the least inclined to laugh at our disguise. Unfortunately I have a beard coming and my voice is breaking. Soon I shall be playing male parts only. Who knows, perhaps one day I shall be playing Hamlet instead of Ophelia!

PRESENTER 1

In playing female characters, Dickie and his young fellow-actors would be greatly helped by the costumes they wore, which could be quite lavish. There was no real attempt to dress the actors in costumes appropriate to the period the play was set in – the costumes were usually Elizabethan ones, whether the play was set in Ancient Greece or medieval Britain. But they would attract and delight the eye of the audience – and they would help to show the status of certain characters, like kings and nobles.

PRESENTER 2

The emphasis on costume made up for the lack of scenery in the Elizabethan theatre. There were no front curtains and the audience could see everything on stage as soon as they entered the theatre. However, the stage was very adaptable and could easily represent a wide range of locations.

PRESENTER 1

The **main stage** was the largest acting area. It was used for battlefields, gardens, open countryside, law courts, rooms in palaces, etc. The **trapdoor** in the centre allowed the occasional ghost to appear from beneath the stage.

PRESENTER 2

The **alcove** at the back could represent a cave, a prison or a throne room, for example. The overhanging **canopy**, held up by the pillars, was painted with the sun, moon and stars and was called 'the heavens'. Through this the machinery in the **hut** could lower thrones or equipment onto the stage below.

PRESENTER 1

Above the alcove was the **balcony**, which was used by musicians as well as by actors. From this balcony Juliet would have made her speech to Romeo in the garden below. It could also be used as the upper window of a house, as the walls of a city, or as a tower.

PRESENTER 2

There were two main **entrances**, one on either side of the stage – convenient for suggesting rival families, as in *Romeo and Juliet* or opposing armies, as in the history plays.

PRESENTER 1

Many scenes could therefore be played on the single stage set, especially since stage properties were extensively used.

PRESENTER 2

A character carrying a torch or a lantern would indicate that the scene took place at night. Tables and chairs were used for taverns and domestic scenes, thrones for royal palaces, artificial trees for gardens.

PRESENTER 1

Often the dramatist would help the audience to imagine a scene by a passage of vivid description.

PRESENTER 2

In *Henry V*, for instance, Shakespeare makes a direct appeal to the audience to use their imagination. He asks, through a speaker called the Chorus:

Can this cockpit hold
The vasty fields of France?

No, of course it can't! He then tells them to imagine what cannot be represented on the stage:

Think, when we talk of horses, that you see them
Printing their proud hoofs i' the receiving earth.

PRESENTER 1

And it worked! The rich descriptive language of Shakespeare's plays, added to the flexible stage, the display of costumes and the wide range of properties, created a theatre that made an immediate and exciting appeal to the mixed audiences.

PRESENTER 2

It is not surprising that the Elizabethan theatre became so popular and produced such fine actors, for the young dramatists of the day wrote plays that have hardly been surpassed for character, language and dramatic effect. Nearly four centuries later, many of these plays are still being performed, not only in this country, but throughout the world.

PRESENTER 1

But the Elizabethan playhouse didn't last for ever and changes were on the way that would transform not only the building and the stage, but the plays and the acting styles as well.

SHAKESPEARE'S THEATRES

In 1608 Shakespeare's company — now called The King's Men because their patron was King James I — bought the lease of a theatre that was inside the city boundary (unlike their main base, The Globe, which was outside official jurisdiction) and began presenting plays there. It was called The Blackfriars Theatre and it differed in many ways from The Globe and the other theatres on the South Bank:

THE BLACKFRIARS

- an indoor theatre; completely enclosed
- performances all the year round
- evening performances
- 6d to enter
- all the audience would be sitting
- audiences tended to be Elizabethan courtiers and professional people
- the stage was at one end of the room
- lighting was by torches hung in brackets along the walls, by candelabra, lanterns and crude footlights along the edge of the stage
- the auditorium measured 66′ by 46′ (approx. 20m × 14m) (including the stage area) — ie it was rectangular
- it could accommodate about 600 spectators

THE GLOBE

- open in the centre
- no performances in winter or during bad weather
- afternoon performances
- 1d (one penny) to enter
- part of the audience would be standing
- audience came from all social classes
- the stage projected into the audience
- there was no lighting; all the performances took place in daylight
- the auditorium was circular or polygonal in shape
- it could hold 2500 – 3000 spectators

The Blackfriars Theatre was a disused monastery hall which had been used for years by companies of boy actors who were also choir boys and had trained voices. The plays they performed always contained music and singing and because the regular audience expected this in plays at The Blackfriars, when The King's Men took it over Shakespeare included more music in his new plays, such as *The Winter's Tale* and *The Tempest*.

What can you see as being the advantages and disadvantages of these contrasting theatres?

23

SOLILOQUIES

- The word *soliloquy* is a combination of two Latin words: *solus*, meaning 'alone', and *loqui*, meaning 'to speak'. One dictionary defines a soliloquy as 'talking to oneself'.

- In a play, a soliloquy is a speech in which a character, alone on the stage, expresses his private thoughts aloud and the audience overhears.

- Soliloquies were often used by Elizabethan dramatists, for they produced a more intimate relationship between the character and the audience, and revealed information that the other characters in the play knew nothing about.

- Many of the soliloquies in Shakespeare's plays occur when a character can't make up his, or her, mind about a particular course of action, such as when Hamlet is debating whether or not to take his own life ('To be, or not to be . . .'); when Macbeth is wavering over killing Duncan; and when Juliet is in two minds whether to drink the potion the Friar has given her.

Here are two contrasting soliloquies, the first Elizabethan, the second modern.

WHAT DO I FEAR? | An extract from *Richard III* by William Shakespeare

RICHARD has committed several murders on his way to the throne. The night before the fatal battle of Bosworth he dreams that the ghosts of his victims visit him and foretell his defeat. When he awakes, it is as if he is split in two – one part feeling guilty for the murders, the other part justifying them.

KING RICHARD

[*The Ghosts vanish.* RICHARD *starts out of his dream.*]
Give me another horse. Bind up my wounds.
Have mercy, Jesu! Soft! I did but dream.
O coward conscience, how dost thou afflict me!
The lights burn blue. It is now dead midnight.
Cold fearful drops stand on my trembling flesh.
What do I fear? Myself? There's none else by.
Richard loves Richard; that is, I am I.
Is there a murderer here? No – yes, I am.
Then fly. What, from myself? Great reason why –
Lest I revenge. What, myself upon myself!
Alack, I love myself. Wherefore? For any good
That I myself have done unto myself?
O, no! Alas, I rather hate myself
For hateful deeds committed by myself!
I am a villain; yet I lie, I am not.
Fool, of thyself speak well. Fool, do not flatter.
My conscience hath a thousand several tongues,
And every tongue brings in a several tale,
And every tale condemns me for a villain.
Perjury, perjury, in the high'st degree;
Murder, stern murder, in the dir'st degree;

> All several sins, all us'd in each degree,
> Throng to the bar, crying all 'Guilty! guilty!'
> I shall despair. There is no creature loves me;
> And if I die no soul will pity me:
> And wherefore should they, since that I myself
> Find in myself no pity to myself?
> Methought the souls of all that I had murder'd
> Came to my tent, and every one did threat
> To-morrow's vengeance on the head of Richard.

THAT'LL TEACH HIM | An extract from *Countdown* by Alan Ayckbourn

The scene takes place after supper, any evening of any week in any year of this 20-year old marriage.

The actual conversation between the HUSBAND and WIFE is printed in **bold**. The other speeches are their thoughts – expressed in soliloquies.

WIFE
His eyes are watering. It's that small print. I knew he needed glasses. If he wasn't so vain. [*He starts to stir his tea.*] Go on, go on stir away. I've had three cups by the time he's finished stirring his first. I wouldn't mind if he'd remembered to put sugar in it. And if he expects me to sugar it for him, just so he can complain it's too sweet...I'm so tired...

HUSBAND
Had an extraordinary dream the other night about a motor mower. Whatever made me? We don't even own a motor mower. No grass. Except for that bit at the side. I suppose that counts as grass. What there is of it. You could cut that with the nail scissors, there's so little of it. Except that I don't think we've got any nail scissors either. I couldn't find them last night for my toe nails. They were catching in the sheet. Serve her right if I'd torn it. She should put things back...bathroom cabinet, second shelf. I put the screw eye in there especially. Then she goes and hangs her sponge bag on it instead, so that the door won't shut, so the mirror's at the wrong angle, so I have to shave with one foot in the bath...I bet she hasn't put any sugar in this...

WIFE
It's not sugared.

HUSBAND
Oh no? Thank you very much. Calmly watches me spraining my wrist stirring the thing...

WIFE
That'll teach him...but maybe I should have told him sooner, now I've got to sit through a second performance.

WRITING A SOLILOQUY

Now you can write a soliloquy, learn it and act it out before the group.

Think about what will make the soliloquy effective: it could be dramatic (like Richard's) or quietly humorous (like Ayckbourn's), but it should aim at creating an interesting character whose thoughts we want to listen to. In what kind of situation would a character express his thoughts aloud to himself? Would there be something on his mind – worrying him, perhaps? What feeling is underlying the thoughts – shame, fear, boredom, pride, guilt, distress? You could begin by improvising.

Linked with the idea of soliloquies is the improvisation 'The Inner Voice' on page 92.

ACTION ON THE STAGE

Shakespeare's plays are not all talk; some scenes are full of action. The limited resources of the Elizabethan stage may have prevented these scenes from achieving their full effect. However, in the modern theatre, through imaginative set designs, lighting and sound effects, they can become visually and dramatically exciting.

One such scene is the opening scene of *The Tempest*, which depicts a ship about to sink in a storm. The crew are represented by the MASTER, the BOATSWAIN and the MARINERS; the passengers by ALONSO, King of Naples, SEBASTIAN, his brother, FERDINAND, his son, ANTONIO, the usurping DUKE OF MILAN, and GONZALO, an old Councillor.

Use this scene, which is given below, as an exercise in planning a production. Consider the various theatrical techniques you could use to create a dramatic opening to the play.

In your discussion, try to answer these questions:

STAGING

What kind of stage would you use?
What suggestions have you for a set design that will represent the ship?
By what means would you try to create the atmosphere of the storm?

Contemporary drawing of The Swan Theatre

ACTING

How would you create a contrast between the ship's crew and the royal passengers?
Where could you make good use of improvisation?
Go through the characters in the scene and define each one (or group) as accurately as you can. What 'type' of actors would you choose for these roles?

After your discussion, perform a workshop rehearsal of the scene.

A PLAGUE UPON THIS HOWLING!

An extract from *The Tempest* by William Shakespeare

ACT 1

SCENE 1: A tempestuous noise of thunder and lightning heard. A ship is seen.

A SHIP-MASTER *and a* BOATSWAIN.

MASTER	Bos'n!
BOATSWAIN	Here, master: what cheer?
MASTER	Good: speak to th'mariners: fall to't—yarely—or we run ourselves aground. Bestir, bestir. [*He goes.*]
	Enter MARINERS.
BOATSWAIN	Heigh my hearts! cheerly, cheerly my hearts...yare, yare...take in the topsail...tend to th'master's whistle...Blow till thou burst thy wind—if room enough! [ALONSO, SEBASTIAN, ANTONIO, FERDINAND, GONZALO, *and others come on deck.*]
ALONSO	Good bos'n, have care. Where's the master? Play the men.
BOATSWAIN	I pray now, keep below.
ANTONIO	Where is the master, bos'n?
BOATSWAIN	Do you not hear him? You mar our labour. Keep your cabins: you do assist the storm.
GONZALO	Nay, good, be patient.
BOATSWAIN	When the sea is. Hence! What care these roarers for the name of king? To cabin! Silence! Trouble us not!
GONZALO	Good, yet remember whom thou hast aboard.

BOATSWAIN	None that I more love than myself. You are a Councillor – if you can command these elements to silence, and work the peace of the present, we will not hand a rope more. Use your authority...If you cannot, give thanks you have lived so long, and make yourself ready in your cabin for the mischance of the hour, if it so hap...Cheerly, good hearts...Out of our way, I say. *[He goes.]*
GONZALO	I have great comfort from this fellow...Methinks he hath no drowning mark upon him, his complexion is perfect gallows. Stand fast, good Fate, to his hanging, make the rope of his destiny our cable, for our own doth little advantage. If he be not born to be hanged, our case is miserable. *[They go below.]*
	[BOATSWAIN returns.]
BOATSWAIN	Down with the topmast...yare, lower, lower! bring her to try with main-course... *[A cry is heard below]* A plague upon this howling...they are louder than the weather, or our office...
	[SEBASTIAN, ANTONIO, and GONZALO return.]
	Yet again? What do you here? Shall we give o'er and drown? Have you a mind to sink?
SEBASTIAN	A pox o' your throat, you bawling, blasphemous, incharitable dog!
BOATSWAIN	Work you, then.
ANTONIO	Hang, cur; hang, you whoreson, insolent noise-maker! We are less afraid to be drowned than thou art.
GONZALO	I'll warrant him for drowning, though the ship were no stronger than a nutshell, and as leaky as an unstaunched wench.
BOATSWAIN	Lay her a-hold, a-hold! Set her two courses. Off to sea again! Lay her off!
	[Enter MARINERS wet.]
MARINERS	All lost! to prayers, to prayers! all lost!
BOATSWAIN	What, must our mouths be cold?
GONZALO	The king and prince at prayers. Let's assist them, For our case is as theirs.
SEBASTIAN	I am out of patience.
ANTONIO	We are merely cheated of our lives by drunkards – This wide-chopped rascal – would thou mightst lie drowning The washing of ten tides!
GONZALO	He'll be hanged yet, Though every drop of water swear against it, And gape at wid'st to glut him.
	[A confused noise below.] Mercy on us! – We split, we split! – Farewell, my wife and children! – Farewell, brother! – We split, we split, we split!
ANTONIO	Let's all sink wi' th' king.
SEBASTIAN	Let's take leave of him
	[They go below.]
GONZALO	Now would I give a thousand furlongs of sea – for an acre of barren ground ... long heath; brown furze, any thing ... The wills above be done, but I would fain die a dry death!

THE DRAMATISTS

The Elizabethan period was the first great flowering of English drama. The theatres that were being built in the London area would not have thrived had it not been for the incredible number of plays that were written and performed during this period. Shakespeare dominates, but Christopher Marlowe and Ben Jonson also have an important place in the history of English drama.

CHRISTOPHER MARLOWE

Born in 1564, the son of a shoemaker, Marlowe was educated at King's School, Canterbury, and at Cambridge University. He had thought of entering the church, but decided to become a writer instead. His reputation was for being rebellious and unconventional, particularly in religious beliefs and he was first an agnostic, then an atheist. His first dramatic success was *Tamburlaine the Great*, an epic of the great Scythian conqueror, written in a blank verse that was described as 'Marlowe's mighty line'. He went on to write plays that had a moral or religious controversy at their centre: *Doctor Faustus, The Jew of Malta* and *Edward II*. His career came to a tragic end when he was killed in a tavern brawl in Deptford at the age of 29.

BEN JONSON

He was born in Westminster and on leaving school went into his stepfather's bricklaying business. As a young man he did voluntary military service in Flanders and when he was 25 he began work for a theatre company as an actor and dramatist. He had a long and varied career (though he suffered a setback when he killed a fellow actor in a duel and had to do a spell in prison) and was a close friend of Shakespeare's. His most successful plays were comedies, but he also wrote tragedies and produced the elaborate musical entertainments called **masques**. He was also a fine poet. He died at the age of 69 and was buried in Westminster Abbey. His best-known plays are: *Every Man in his Humour* (which, on its first production, had Shakespeare in the cast), *Sejanus, Volpone, The Alchemist, Bartholomew Fair* and *The Devil is an Ass*.

WILLIAM SHAKESPEARE

We often speak of Shakespeare as being an 'Elizabethan' dramatist – as he was. But we ought to remember that he was also a Jacobean dramatist, for he continued to write after Elizabeth's death into the first ten years of James I's reign. His birthplace was Stratford upon Avon in 1564 and he was educated at the local grammar school. He left when he was about 15, married when he was 18 (to Anne Hathaway, eight years his senior) and by 20 was the father of three children. A few years later he left Stratford for London (though he returned frequently throughout his career). He became an actor, then a writer in the Lord Chamberlain's company. Though his early plays were performed in several theatres, the main body of his work was produced at The Globe on the South Bank. He wrote 34 plays and collaborated with other dramatists to write three others. He retired from the theatre after writing *The Tempest* and settled in Stratford. He died in 1616 and was buried in Holy Trinity church, Stratford, where 52 years earlier, he had been christened. After his death two of his friends from the Lord Chamberlain's Men (and later the King's Men), collected his plays and published them in one volume. This is referred to as the First Folio.

STUDY TOPICS

The Globe Theatre
Elizabethan boy-actors
A biography of Marlowe, Jonson or
    Shakespeare
Elizabethan acting companies

Richard Burbage
The Elizabethan audience
Shakespeare productions today
The Royal Shakespeare Company

Teachers keep telling us that Shakespeare is still relevant today – he deals with racial prejudice in *The Merchant of Venice*, young love in *Romeo and Juliet* and dictatorship in *Julius Caesar*. Well, I haven't read all these plays and I'm prepared to admit that he has something to say on modern topics, but when he wraps it up in such complicated plots and heavy language, it just doesn't come across – to me, anyway!

JOIN THE DISCUSSION ON . . . SHAKESPEARE

You can only judge Shakespeare by what you've seen or read – and even then, when you've seen a play and come away feeling it was awful, you have to decide whether Shakespeare was to blame, or the director or the actors – or even you, yourself! I've seen a brilliant production of *Hamlet* and a terrible one. Where does that leave Shakespeare?

I decided to watch all the plays in the Shakespeare television series, so that I would know something about every one and become a sort of expert. After the third one I gave up – and I was sitting down in the living room! Just think of all those groundlings who actually *stood* for three hours – in the open air, as well – to watch the plays! What did they see in Shakespeare that I'm missing?

Who wants social relevance? I don't go to the theatre to be given lessons in sociology or politics, or even the psychology of young love. I go to be entertained and Shakespeare *is* entertaining, if you choose the right play. I don't think I'd want to see *Henry VI, Parts 1, 2* and *3* very often, but I'd go to a performance of *Twelfth Night* any day!

It was live. Shakespeare live is different from Shakespeare on the box. But even so, at least they could see the actors easily and hear what was being said. We went to Stratford to see *Macbeth* last year and we were in the gallery but we were so far back you had to strain to hear and you needed a telescope to see what was going on! Whoever built that place didn't know anything about theatres! At least the Elizabethans knew how to build theatres that not only gave the actors a chance, but let the audience feel part of the play as well. And at a penny a time, they were cheap, which is more than they are nowadays.

The Royal Shakespeare Company is heavily subsidised by the government through the Arts Council, of course, otherwise they couldn't make ends meet. Do you think there would be so many productions of Shakespeare if there were no subsidy and it was left to the commercial theatre to keep the plays alive? Would it matter, do you think?

The Restoration and After

PRESENTER 1
1642 to 1660 was the period of the Commonwealth, when England was ruled by a Puritan parliament led by Oliver Cromwell. King Charles I had been executed and his son, Charles II, was in exile in France.

PRESENTER 2
On taking power, the Puritans issued an order declaring that public stage plays had to cease forthwith and that all actors were to be considered rogues. The theatres that remained were demolished.

PRESENTER 1
It meant, of course, that actors went 'underground' and performed plays secretly in inns and private houses, but at the risk of being arrested in mid-performance and imprisoned. Theatre such as the Elizabethans had known ceased to exist – as well as bear-baiting, cockfighting and dancing round the maypole.

PRESENTER 2
In 1660, however, Charles II was restored to the throne and one of his first acts was to revive the theatre. It was the beginning of what we call the Restoration Theatre, which proved to be radically different from the theatres that had preceded it.

PRESENTER 1
The man at the centre of the changes was Thomas Killigrew. He had been a pageboy to Charles I, and was a successful dramatist in the years before the Puritans closed the theatres. He had been at the court of the exiled king in France, and on his return was made Groom of the Royal Bedchamber. He seems a suitable person to introduce us to the Restoration Theatre.

THOMAS
In France the court became accustomed to visiting the theatres. They were roofed and had special boxes for people of quality. The King could easily be seen and his dignity maintained. The plays – particularly those by Molière – were so brilliant and amusing! We rather thought we would like to establish this kind of theatre in London and on our return we set about it. I started off by converting a tennis court in Vere Street, but went on to build the Theatre Royal in Drury Lane, incorporating many new ideas. It was a rectangular theatre – not like Shakespeare's Wooden O. The stage was framed by a proscenium arch, in front of which was the semi-circular **apron** which allowed the actors to approach nearer the audience. There was moveable scenery at the back of the stage so that we could suggest different scenes. The stage and the auditorium were lit by numerous candles in beautiful chandeliers. Above all, everything was well-ordered and civil, quite unlike the bear garden we used to have in the old days! A theatre to be proud of!

Interior of Drury Lane Theatre

31

PRESENTER 2

Well, not entirely! Thomas *did* introduce many exciting changes, but he hasn't yet mentioned the **Patents**. These did much to hold back the development of the theatre in the 17th and 18th centuries. Don't imagine that, now the Puritans were out of the way, just anyone could open a theatre and put on a play!

THOMAS

Of course, though the King was extremely anxious to revive the theatre, he felt he ought to exercise some control over what was actually presented. I mean, for political reasons, he couldn't allow a free-for-all and run the risk of dramatists ridiculing the Monarchy, could he? He decided, therefore, that theatres should be properly licensed, or given Royal Patents, to permit them to operate with official approval. He issued two in all, and I'm pleased to say that I was the recipient of one of them. The other went to my old friend William Davenant, Shakespeare's godson, who had also been with Charles in exile. I founded the King's Company in Drury Lane, whilst William formed the Duke's Company, the Duke of York being the future James II, and opened his theatre in Dorset Gardens. Eventually this gave rise to the Theatre Royal, Covent Garden. Together we established the two theatres that were to be the chief source of theatrical entertainment for the next 22 years. Not a minor achievement in theatrical history, you might think!

PRESENTER 1

On the other hand, you might think it wasn't much of an advance on the Puritan restriction! But, as in the Commonwealth period, there were producers, writers and actors who put on plays without official approval. The Royal Patents, however, lasted quite some time. They weren't abolished till 1843.

PRESENTER 2

Not long after Thomas Killigrew opened the Theatre Royal a young girl aged about 14 was employed as an orange-seller there. Her name was Nell Gwynne. Like Nell, many girls found social advancement in the Restoration Theatre, where fashionable people went more to view one another than to see the play. Let's hear from Annie, another attractive young orange-seller from the 1660s:

Thomas Killigrew

ANNIE

We don't only sell oranges, you know. We sell lemons, sweetmeats, fruit and nuts as well. But mostly oranges – which some of the customers guzzle during the play and then throw the skins on the floor for us to slip on! There's so much noise and to-ing and fro-ing I don't know how the actors can stand it! Some of the audience up on the stage chat away to each other and even shout down to their friends. I don't think much of that. It's only when a great actor like Mr Betterton or a beauty like Nell Gwynne is on the stage that everyone watches the play! Nell Gwynne was an orange girl once. Now look where she is – the King's mistress! (Well, *one* of them, anyway!) I sometimes say to myself, if she can do it, why can't you, Annie? Them young fops in the boxes often wink and nod at me when I pass by with my basket. But, mind you, Nell was good-looking, and though she could hardly write her name, she must have had *something* to get her so far. I don't think I'm cut out to mix with royalty somehow . . . oranges . . . lemons . . . fruit . . . nuts . . . lovely oranges!

PRESENTER 1

Did you notice that Annie spoke of Nell Gwynne being 'on the stage'? A woman – on the stage? An *actress*! There were no actresses in the

Elizabethan and Jacobean theatres. All the female roles were taken by boys. This was something new. It had been decreed by Charles II, who said that all female parts *must* be acted by women! It was the beginning of a new era in theatrical history. The first actress to appear on the English stage was Margaret Hughes, who played Desdemona in a production of *Othello*.

PRESENTER 2
The audience, however, was kept in total ignorance until the beginning of the play when an actor made this announcement:

I come, unknown to any of the rest,
To tell you news: I saw the lady dressed.
The woman plays today, mistake me not,
No man in gown, or page in petticoat.

PRESENTER 1
Margaret Hughes opened the way for a succession of highly talented actresses in the 17th and 18th centuries – women like Peg Woffington (who, ironically enough, excelled at playing men's parts!) and the famous Mrs Siddons.

PRESENTER 2
There may not have been a Women's Movement during the Restoration, but women were certainly asserting their right to be seen and heard – seen as actresses and heard as dramatists. For yet another 'first' was chalked up in the 1660s – the first woman playwright to have a play produced on the London stage. She was Katherine Philips, better known as 'The Matchless Orinda', and her play was called *Pompey*.

PRESENTER 1
The most successful of women dramatists at this time, however, was Aphra Behn. She not only wrote as well as many of the men, but dealt with subjects that concerned women of the time, such as arranged marriages which she tackled in *The Rover*.

PRESENTER 2
At first, however, the theatre managers were content to specialise in revivals of older plays. They preferred merry comedies, but when they did choose a tragedy they often gave it an unexpected twist, in keeping with the mood of the day. So Romeo and Juliet lived happily ever after; King Lear ended the play blissfully hand in hand with Cordelia and the Witches in *Macbeth* became singing sisters.

PRESENTER 1
Tragedies written in the period were far outclassed by the comedies, with their witty and cynical dialogue, their convoluted plots of sex and intrigue, and their brilliant caricatures of contemporary types.

PRESENTER 2
You can get some idea of the plays from their titles; typical ones were: *The Careless Husband, Love in a Tub* and *She Would if She Could*.

PRESENTER 1
These **comedies of manners** as they were later to be called, were highly entertaining and didn't offend anyone in authority. But then a different kind of play began to creep into the theatre. It was political satire and it produced another 'first' – the **Censor**.

PRESENTER 2
The Censor was created as a direct result of Henry Fielding's plays. Fielding, better known for his novels *Tom Jones* and *Joseph Andrews*, was a clever, outspoken writer. He took over the management of The Little Theatre in the Hay, now The Haymarket in London, in order to present some of his recent plays. But let the Lord Chamberlain take up the story:

THE LORD CHAMBERLAIN
You know, of course, that the Lord Chamberlain *is* the Censor? Well, we didn't want to introduce censorship. We would have preferred the playwrights to be absolutely free to express whatever they chose; but when Henry Fielding began to take the law into his own hands, we had to act. He had taken over the management of The Little Theatre in the Hay – an unpatented theatre and therefore quite illegal. Not only that, he had written and presented offensive, diabolical satires suggesting that there was bribery and corruption during county elections – a vile slur on a government which, as you know, scrupulously ensured that all elections were conducted with absolute fairness! The plays were so popular they ran for 50 performances! Not satisfied with that, Mr Fielding then wrote a play that poured ridicule and abuse on the Prime Minister himself. Not

directly, of course, but through the character of Quidam, a fiddler who bribed people to dance to the tunes he played. Well, the parallel was obvious. Sir Robert Walpole was furious and he immediately drew up a bill which gave the Lord Chamberlain power to refuse a licence to any play he disapproved of. Needless to say, as soon as the Act was passed The Little Theatre in the Hay was closed and Mr Fielding was . . . out on the street! I believe he took to writing novels.

Of course, the result of the Act was extremely beneficial. It meant that dramatists could concentrate on comedies of social manners (which we all find so amusing!) and leave politics to the politicians! As Lord Chamberlain I have a duty to protect our rulers from vicious attacks by irresponsible writers. The theatre has proved a healthier place since the Censor began his work! Long may it remain so!

PRESENTER 1
It did long remain so. The office of Censor was not abolished till 1968!

PRESENTER 2
But what the Censor couldn't prohibit was fine acting and the 18th century produced in David Garrick an actor who became legendary – he has been described as 'the first superstar of the English theatre'.

PRESENTER 1
Garrick was born at Hereford in 1717, the son of an army officer. At 19 he was sent to an academy near Lichfield run by Samuel Johnson. But the academy proved unsuccessful and both teacher and pupil decided to set off for London, with hardly a penny in their pockets.

PRESENTER 2
They remained friends for the rest of their lives and both found fame in different spheres. Garrick became a law student, but gave it up and went into the wine trade. This took him into the company of actors, many of whom performed in inns, and through an actor named Charles Macklin ('Wicked Charlie'), Garrick first took to the boards – as a stand-in for the part of Harlequin, the traditional comic character.

PRESENTER 1
After a season in the provinces he was offered the title role in Shakespeare's *Richard III* in London. He created a sensation. All 150 performances were a sell-out. 'Extraordinary and great,' said one commentator. 'That young man never had his equal as an actor and will never have a rival,' said Alexander Pope, the most famous poet of his day. Some praise for an actor at the beginning of his career!

PRESENTER 2
But Garrick's genius showed itself not only in his acting. He was a great all-rounder – dramatist, manager, director and theatrical reformer – at a time when the theatre needed to be shaken-up. How can a man with such talents speak about himself without appearing immodest? 'Little Davy', as he was affectionately called, will try:

DAVID GARRICK
You must believe me when I say the London theatre was in a terrible mess! Chaos reigned – on stage, backstage and in the auditorium! When I took over the management of Drury Lane, I tried to improve things. First, the actors: I got them to attend rehearsals regularly and punctually, to know their parts *before* the opening night, and to act in a more natural style, instead of the pompous voices, the popping eyeballs and exaggerated gestures that were the current fashion. Then there was the audience – especially your fashionable

'The Laughing Audience' by Hogarth

beaux – dallying with the actresses in their dressing rooms. Even during the performance, they packed the stage so that an actor could scarcely move. When Mrs Cibber played Juliet, she had a hundred of the audience in the tomb with her! I cleared them off the stage and confined their backstage visits to after the final curtain. And we discontinued the practice of charging half-price to anyone who arrived after the interval or left early!

Garrick as Macbeth

Then there was the question of the stage itself. What use was the apron? It thrust the actor into the audience, but it left the stage proper empty and unused. My answer was to cut the apron strings – to use that space for extra seating and to put the actor behind the proscenium arch. We recruited artists from the Continent to design scenery which could be slid on and off to create new scenes. To give even more importance to the stage itself, we darkened the auditorium and lit the stage by footlights and side-lights – not with the smoky candles, but with oil lamps. There was opposition all along the way, but the hard work was undoubtedly worthwhile.

PRESENTER 1

In spite of his dynamic energy, Garrick was feeling the strain of being theatre manager, producer and a leading actor. In 1775 he announced that he was retiring from the stage, but would give a series of farewell performances in each of his famous roles. There was a rush to get seats from all sections of the population. Hannah More, a writer of the day, wrote:

The eagerness of people to see him is beyond anything you can have idea of. You will see half a dozen duchesses and countesses of a night in the upper boxes: for the fear of not seeing him at all has humbled those who used to go not for the purpose of seeing as being seen – and

now they curtsey to the ground for the worst places in the house.

PRESENTER 2

Garrick died at 61 and was buried in Westminster Abbey. A memorial to him was erected in Lichfield Cathedral, inscribed with an epitaph written by his old friend Dr Johnson:

I am disappointed by the stroke of death which has eclipsed the gaiety of nations and impoverished the public stock of harmless pleasure.

PRESENTER 1

The theatre that Garrick had sought to revitalise produced some of the finest comedies in the language, especially *She Stoops to Conquer* by Oliver Goldsmith and *The Rivals* by Richard Brindsley Sheridan, who actually succeeded Garrick as manager of the Theatre Royal. These comedies had a gentle humour and less cynicism than those of the Restoration and they ended a great era in theatrical history.

Getting the facts right

1 What were the dates of the Commonwealth?
2 Why is the theatre called the *Restoration* Theatre?
3 What was a Royal Patent?
4 Who received the first Royal Patents?
5 Which theatres became the main official theatres in the 17th and 18th centuries?
6 When was the Patent abolished?
7 Which French dramatist influenced Restoration comedy?
8 What was a 'proscenium arch'?
9 What was the 'apron'?
10 Who was the first actress on the English stage?
11 What part did she play?
12 Who was the first woman dramatist?
13 What was Garrick's nickname?
14 In which role did he first achieve fame?
15 Which two famous comedies were written towards the end of the 18th century?

QUESTIONS TO CONSIDER

- Do you think it mattered that Shakespeare's plays were altered?

- Can you see any reason why women should play men's roles in the 17th century?

- What do you think of stage censorship? Is there an argument for bringing it back?

- What advantages and disadvantages were there in the system of Royal Patents?

- What were the main reforms that Garrick introduced? Which were the most important and which the least?

- Why do you think audiences were so rowdy in the 18th century? Why do audiences tend to be 'polite' in our own day? Ought we to be more outspoken at the theatre?

MORE DETAILED STUDY

You might find it interesting to study one or more of the figures in Restoration and 18th-century theatre in more depth. Using biographies and encyclopedias, try to build up a portrait of one of these characters:

Nell Gwynne
Mrs Siddons
Aphra Behn
Oliver Goldsmith
Henry Fielding
David Garrick
Richard Brindsley Sheridan

National Theatre production of *The Rivals*

FORGET THIS FELLOW!

An extract from *The Rivals* by Richard Sheridan

Sheridan, like the Restoration dramatists, reflected the society he lived in: the world of fashion, intrigue, elopement and marriage.

The Rivals was Sheridan's first play, written when he was 24, and produced at the Covent Garden Theatre in 1775. Its theme is love and marriage, seen from the angle of rebellious youth.

LYDIA LANGUISH is in love with ENSIGN BEVERLEY, but her aunt and guardian, MRS MALAPROP, insists on her marrying CAPTAIN ABSOLUTE. However, unknown to either of these ladies, Ensign Beverley and Captain Absolute are the same person.

In this scene, Lydia shows her rebellious spirit and Mrs Malaprop and SIR ANTHONY ABSOLUTE express their disapproval of the youth of their day. Lydia has just hidden the books she does not want her aunt to see she is reading and has left *Fordyce's Sermons* open on the table.

[*Enter* MRS MALAPROP *and* SIR ANTHONY ABSOLUTE.]

MRS MALAPROP There, Sir Anthony, there sits the deliberate Simpleton, who wants to disgrace her family, and lavish herself on a fellow not worth a shilling!

LYDIA Madam, I thought you once –

MRS MALAPROP You thought, Miss! – I don't know any business you have to think at all – thought does not become a young woman. But the point we would request of you is, that you will promise to forget this fellow – to illiterate him, I say, quite from your memory.

LYDIA Ah! Madam! our memories are independent of our wills. – It is not so easy to forget.

MRS MALAPROP But I say it is, Miss; there is nothing on earth so easy as to *forget*, if a person chooses to set about it. – I'm sure I have as much forgot your poor dear uncle as if he had never existed – and I thought it my duty so to do; and let me tell you, Lydia, these violent memories don't become a young woman.

SIR ANTHONY Why sure she won't pretend to remember what she's order'd not! – aye, this comes of her reading!

LYDIA What crime, Madam, have I committed to be treated thus?

MRS MALAPROP Now don't attempt to extirpate yourself from the matter; you know I have proof controvertible of it. – But tell me, will you promise to do as you're bid? – Will you take a husband of your friend's choosing?

LYDIA Madam, I must tell you plainly, that had I no preference for any one else, the choice you have made would be my aversion.

MRS MALAPROP What business have you, Miss, with *preference* and *aversion?* They don't become a young woman; and you ought to know, that as both always wear off, 'tis safest in matrimony to begin with a little *aversion*. I am sure I hated your poor dear

	uncle before marriage as if he'd been a black-a-moor – and yet, Miss, you are sensible what a wife I made! – and when it pleas'd Heav'n to release me from him, 'tis unknown what tears I shed! – But suppose we were going to give you another choice, will you promise us to give up this Beverley?
LYDIA	Could I belie my thoughts so far, as to give that promise, my actions would certainly as far belie my words.
MRS MALAPROP	Take yourself to your room. – You are fit company for nothing but your own ill-humours.
LYDIA	Willingly, Ma'am – I cannot change for the worse.

[*Exit* LYDIA.]

MRS MALAPROP	There's a little intricate hussy for you!
SIR ANTHONY	It is not to be wonder'd at, Ma'am – all this is the natural consequence of teaching girls to read. – Had I a thousand daughters, by Heaven! I'd as soon have them taught the black-art as their alphabet!
MRS MALAPROP	Nay, nay, Sir Anthony, you are an absolute misanthropy.
SIR ANTHONY	In my way hither, Mrs Malaprop, I observed your niece's maid coming forth from a circulating library! – She had a book in each hand – they were half-bound volumes, with marble covers! – From that moment I guess'd how full of duty I should see her mistress!
MRS MALAPROP	Those are vile places, indeed!
SIR ANTHONY	Madam, a circulating library in a town is, as an ever-green tree, of diabolical knowledge! – It blossoms through the year! – And depend on it, Mrs Malaprop, that they who are so fond of handling the leaves, will long for the fruit at last.
MRS MALAPROP	Fie, fie, Sir Anthony, you surely speak laconically!
SIR ANTHONY	Why, Mrs Malaprop, in moderation, now, what would you have a woman know?
MRS MALAPROP	Observe me, Sir Anthony. – I would by no means wish a daughter of mine to be a progeny of learning; I don't think so much learning becomes a young woman; for instance – I would never let her meddle with Greek, or Hebrew, or Algebra, or Simony, or Fluxions, or Paradoxes, or such inflammatory branches of learning – neither would it be necessary for her to handle any of your mathematical, astronomical, diabolical instruments; – But, Sir Anthony, I would send her, at nine years old, to a boarding-school, in order to learn a little ingenuity and artifice. – Then, Sir, she should have a supercilious knowledge in accounts; – and as she grew up, I would have her instructed in geometry, that she might know something of the contagious countries; – but above all, Sir Anthony, she should be mistress of orthodoxy, that she might not mis-spell, and mis-pronounce words so shamefully as girls usually do; and likewise that she might reprehend the true meaning of what she is saying. – This, Sir Anthony, is what I would have a woman know; – and I don't think there is a superstitious article in it.
SIR ANTHONY	Well, well, Mrs Malaprop, I will dispute the point no further with you; though I must confess, that you are a truly moderate and polite arguer, for almost every third word you say is on my side of the question. – But, Mrs Malaprop, to

	the more important point in debate, – you say, you have no objection to my proposal.
MRS MALAPROP	None, I assure you. – I am under no positive engagement with Mr Acres, and as Lydia is so obstinate against him, perhaps your son may have better success.
SIR ANTHONY	Well, Madam, I will write for the boy directly. – He knows not a syllable of this yet, though I have for some time had the proposal in my head. He is at present with his regiment.
MRS MALAPROP	We have never seen your son, Sir Anthony; but I hope no objection on his side.
SIR ANTHONY	Objection! – let him object if he dare! – No, no, Mrs Malaprop, Jack knows that the least demur puts me in a frenzy directly. – My process was always very simple – in their younger days, 'twas 'Jack, do this,' – if he demur'd – I knock'd him down – and if he grumbled at that – I always sent him out of the room.
MRS MALAPROP	Aye, and the properest way, o' my conscience! – nothing is so conciliating to young people as severity. – Well, Sir Anthony, I shall give Mr Acres his discharge, and prepare Lydia to receive you son's invocations; – and I hope you will represent *her* to the Captain as an object not altogether illegible.
SIR ANTHONY	Madam, I will handle the subject prudently. – Well, I must leave you – and let me beg you, Mrs Malaprop, to enforce this matter roundly to the girl; – take my advice – keep a tight hand – if she rejects this proposal – clap her under lock and key: – and if you were just to let the servants forget to bring her dinner for three or four days, you can't conceive how she'd come about. [*Exit* SIR ANTHONY.]

ACTING THE SCENE

To act in 18th-century comedy requires a style and technique quite different from the naturalism associated with plays of our own day. Movements, gestures, facial expressions, accents and tones of voice should all be studied. These convey the social mannerisms of the 18th-century upper class and bring out the oddities of individual characters.

Work through the scene, experimenting with stage business and acting style appropriate to the period. How would you bring out the contrast between the young and the older characters? What degree of caricature would you allow to Mrs Malaprop and Sir Anthony? Where exactly does the comedy lie in the scenes and how would you make the most of it?

IMPROVISATION

This scene illustrates the attitude of the older generation to the younger one. Things are hardly the same today: we seldom get parents choosing the spouses for their sons and daughters. Yet parallels do exist in that older members of a family often try to force their will on the younger members, sometimes with bitter consequences.

Can you think of examples of this type of situation? When you have talked it over, sketch out an improvisation to dramatise the idea, but decide first whether you should treat it in a serious or a comic manner. Sheridan criticises Mrs Malaprop and Sir Anthony by making us laugh at them. You might try doing the same with your adult characters – or your young ones!

You will find more ideas for improvisation on this theme in 'Parents and Children' on page 90.

THE THEATRE CRITIC

The 18th century saw the first appearance of the theatre critic. Actors, actresses, playwrights and producers all disapproved of him and they haven't changed their minds since. To many people the critic is a sponger, earning his living from the talents and artistic efforts of others. But he is also a necessary medium between the play on the stage and the general public, when he conveys information and gives a considered opinion based on taste and sound judgment.

Here is the *Evening Standard* review of a production of Goldsmith's popular Restoration comedy, *She Stoops to Conquer*. It will help us to answer the questions: **What is the purpose of a review? What is the function of a critic?**

ANY list of great English playwrights will include the name of Oliver Goldsmith. Yet he wrote only one well-known play, **She Stoops to Conquer**, and it is in truth a rather small thing to be commended for its affectionate charm rather than either its language, its wit or its significance.

Giles Block's production at the **Lyttelton** has wisely allowed it to meander along its uncomplicated way, encouraging us to be entranced by its simple account of love triumphant over a case of mistaken identity.

A marriage has been proposed between the young Marlow and Kate Hardcastle, the daughter of a rich provincial landowner, and on Marlow's way, with his friend Hastings, to meet his suggested bride for the first time, the two young men get lost.

At a local inn, they meet Hardcastle's stepson, Tony Lumpkin who, as a practical joke, directs Marlow and Hastings to spend the night at a neighbouring hostelry which is in reality, Hardcastle's spacious home.

It seems that the same trick had once been played on Goldsmith himself.

Marlow's problem is that he is desperately bashful and begins to stutter when he is in the presence of any respectable young girl and can only display his natural lascivious tastes when he is in a brothel or trying to seduce females of the lower orders.

The comedy that emerges is based upon the social snobbery of the period with Marlow making an ass of himself by treating his bewildered host with contemptuous disdain while finding himself intrigued by Kate, whom he mistakes for a servant girl.

Dressed by Alison Chitty as if they had just stepped out of a Hogarth painting, these 18th-century characters plot, prattle and pout their way through a succession of amiable misunderstandings until love finally breaks through to provide a wholesome and jolly ending.

Since Goldsmith relies upon good-natured fun rather than either brittle dialogue or cynical observation to achieve his effects, there are times during the leisurely unwinding of the action when one's interest droops to a somnolent level.

Tony Lumpkin, whose presence usually provides some outrageous farce to the proceedings, is deprived by Tony Haygarth's interpretation of much of his extreme obnoxiousness, leaving a more credible but less amusing character behind.

The Hardcastles, as represented by a twittering Dora Bryan and a combustible Tom Baker, have their moments of apoplectic delight.

Hywell Bennett is a strangely subdued Marlow who never quite reflects either a tongue-tied swell or a swaggering rake. Julia Watson as Kate is pleasingly flighty and provocative.

For 'O'-level students this uncluttered production will undoubtedly be a great help. Their parents may want something sharper.

Milton Shulman

1 Say whether or not you would want to see the play after reading this review.
2 What part of the review is not concerned with the critic's opinion of the play?
3 How important do you think this part of the review is?
4 What aspects of the production are not mentioned? How important are they in a review?
5 Quote some examples of the reviewer's criticism of the play itself and of the acting.
6 Do you accept the final remark about students and their parents?
7 On the whole, do you think the critic has the right approach to reviewing a play or not?

Critics can 'kill' a play by their reviews. Should they?

WRITING A CRITICAL REVIEW

As part of your drama work you will probably visit a theatre and be asked to write a review of the play you saw. On this occasion you will be a critic, passing judgment on the individuals and groups of people whose efforts have put the play on the stage: playwright, director, actors, set designer, costume designer, lighting expert and other specialists. You may not want to comment on every aspect of the production, but it might help you to put your ideas into order if you followed a structural outline for your review such as this:

1 INTRODUCTION

Title of play: *You Can't Take It With You*
Authors: Kaufman and Hart
Theatre: National Theatre, South Bank, London

After the factual information, your review could begin with one of the following:
– the impression you had of the theatre;
– background information on the play and the playwright;
– personal feelings about going to the theatre;
– the curtain going up on the first scene.

2 THE SET

Some stage sets are extremely elaborate, others are little more than a bare stage. Your question is: how appropriate is the set to the play that is being staged? In *You Can't Take It With You* the set was a realistically detailed interior of a New York house, with a staircase to the first floor, a large hall and living room, doors to kitchen and cellar – as well as a backcloth depicting the buildings and streets of New York. It got a round of applause when the curtain went up.
Judgment: brilliant – absolutely convincing, right down to the 1930s typewriter.

3 THE PLAY

Give a brief outline of the play. On the whole, was it a success? Try to identify the parts that worked well. Did it hold the audience's interest? Was their response good? Where did the 'drama' actually lie? Was the play pure entertainment, or did it have a 'message'? If so, did you agree with it – and was it integrated into the action of the play? What about the characters? Were they credible?

4 THE ACTING

You will obviously have liked some performers more than others. Give one or two examples of successful acting styles – of the use of mannerisms, voice, gesture and movement. If you thought the acting was weak in places, was it the fault of the actor or the dramatist? How well were the main parts played? Were there any minor roles you thought were acted brilliantly?

5 CONCLUSION

Your impressions of a play cannot all be put under neat headings. Bring in anything you thought remarkably good or bad about the play, the production and the performances. On balance, was it a successful piece of theatre. Did it keep your attention? Did it make you want to know what happened next? Did it make you laugh, weep, think? Don't fall into the critics' trap of being superior!

Make good use of the theatre programme for factual information.

The Nineteenth Century

PRESENTER 1

This was the century of the great actor rather than the great dramatist.

PRESENTER 2

Perhaps good writers were put off the theatre by the heavy presence of our old friend the Lord Chamberlain, who censored anything that smacked of liberal thinking in politics, religion and social questions.

PRESENTER 1

And at the beginning of the century, the theatre was still looked down upon by some sections of society. Allardyce Nicoll, the drama historian, sums up the situation like this:

> Sane, sober people who might have helped the growth of a finer drama were obliged to keep themselves aloof . . . Prostitutes thronged the foyers; coarse language, rioting, drunkenness abounded.

The clown Grimaldi

Charles Kean, in an attempt to reassure his respectable patrons, advertised that 'all the policemen selected for duty are members of the Church of England', while the linkman was a distinguished member of the Baptist church!

PRESENTER 2

The two 'official' theatres – Covent Garden and Drury Lane – also discouraged new drama. They were large, cavernous places where actors had to shout to be heard. They were much better suited to opera and musicals, which is what they eventually specialised in. Even today, Drury Lane is the London home of the big American musicals, like *42nd Street*.

PRESENTER 1

Yet, oddly enough, these two theatres were the only theatres permitted to perform 'straight' plays. In every other theatre a play could only be performed if it was accompanied by music! The way round this was to have a piano tinkling away throughout the performance, or to have at least five songs in each act of the play.

PRESENTER 2

Even Shakespeare could be illegal! A theatre in Shoreditch was raided and the entire cast plus 80 members of the audience were marched through the streets to the police station. Their crime was being involved in a production of *Othello*!

PRESENTER 1

What usually happened was that these 'minor' theatres, as they were called, presented pantomimes, ballets and even performing animals, or put on plays called **burlettas** which contained the required amount of music and song.

PRESENTER 2

All this because of the Patents Act of 1660,

Lost in London – a Victorian melodrama

which was still in force. Naturally there was an energetic campaign to have the Act abolished and give the minor theatres their artistic freedom. Eventually in 1843 a new Act was passed that removed the privileges from Covent Garden and Drury Lane and freed the minor theatres from their restrictions. Said Sam Lane to his largely working-class audience in The Britannia, Hoxton: 'I am proud to have helped in this success in obtaining freedom for the people's amusement. Never again will you be deprived of free theatre!' Sam had reason to rejoice. He had lost his licence for staging a straight production of one of the most popular Victorian plays, *Black-Eyed Susan*.

PRESENTER 1

Black-Eyed Susan was a **melodrama** – a word we haven't met before in our study of the theatre. It is now almost a term of sarcasm for a play with an overdramatic plot, oversimplified characters and outsize emotions. Although the Victorian melodramas had these characteristics, they also had their roots in the domestic lives and occupations of the age itself. In fact, they introduced a new character into English drama – the working-class hero.

PRESENTER 2

The early melodramas thrilled their audiences with lurid tales told against a backdrop of ruined abbeys, dark dungeons and mysterious temples; but as the century developed, the themes touched more and more upon the lives of ordinary people of all classes in contemporary England. They remained true, however, to the staple ingredients of melodrama, with their wicked villains, high-minded heroes and pure-hearted heroines. Dastardly deeds, guilty secrets, long-lost lovers, abandoned children, extortionate landlords and happy endings were guaranteed to make the audience gasp and weep. It was a truly 'popular' theatre that attracted large audiences throughout the country.

PRESENTER 1

Here's an extract from the melodrama *The Vampire; or, The Bride of the Isles*, first performed in 1820. The wicked RUTHVEN, Earl of Marsden, carries off young EFFIE, intending to marry her. Effie's betrothed, ROBERT, sees the abduction and rushes off in pursuit. Also involved are ANDREW, Effie's father and LORD RONALD, Ruthven's friend.

NO POWER ON EARTH

An extract from *The Vampire; or, The Bride of the Isles*

Scene: Garden of Lord Ruthven's Castle: the sea in the background.

EFFIE	My lord, I'll hear no more – If Robert –
RUTHVEN	Think not of him; my bride thou art – no power on earth shall tear thee from me: say, Effie, that you love me. *[Taking her hand.]*
EFFIE	*[Starting]* Mercy on me! – My lord, I – I know not what to say. My heart beats so that – Oh, pray leave me, my lord. *[Sobbing.]*
RUTHVEN	This instant let me bear thee to the priest.
EFFIE	My lord, for pity's sake –
RUTHVEN	You plead in vain: – Effie, thou art mine for ever. *[Bears her off. Re-enter* ROBERT.*]*
ROBERT	How long she stays – Not here! Why, [EFFIE *shrieks.*] Heav'ns! what do I see – borne off and struggling – Villain, loose your hold! *[Draws a pistol and runs after them. Enter* ANDREW *and* LORD RONALD.*]*
RONALD	Why, Andrew, said you not the Earl was here?
ANDREW	'Twas here I left him but just now, my lord. *[A pistol is fired without, and* EFFIE *shrieks, 'O save me! Save me!']*
ANDREW	My daughter's voice! *[Rushes out, as* LORD RUTHVEN *enters wounded.]*
RONALD	Ruthven!
RUTHVEN	*[Falling]* I die!
RONALD	What murderous hand –
RUTHVEN	Exclaim not. I have but a moment to live. Ronald, swear by the host of heaven to obey my last commands.
RONALD	I do, I do. – I swear by all that is most dear and sacred to honour and to man, to fulfil your last desire.
RUTHVEN	Conceal my death from every human being, till yonder moon shall be set this night: and 'ere an hour shall elapse after I have expired, throw this ring into the waves that wash the tomb of Fingal.
RONALD	I will, I will, Ruthven! – Dear Ruthven.
RUTHVEN	Remember your oath. The lamp of night is descending the blue heavens: when I am dead, let its sweet light shine on me. – Farewell. Remember – Remember your oath. *[Dies.]* *[Solemn music.* RONALD *lays the body of* RUTHVEN *on a bank in the garden, and kneels mournfully beside it.]*

PRESENTER 2

Save your tears! He's not really dead. And he's the Vampire, anyway! He survives till the end of the play when, quite rightly, he's struck by a thunderbolt and vanishes!

PRESENTER 1

There were many such scenes in Victorian melodrama. In fact, the demand exceeded the supply. Some theatres even had resident dramatists who turned out melodramas by the dozen and popular novels were plundered for plots, particularly those of Charles Dickens and Walter Scott. In 1819 there were no fewer than six separate versions of Scott's *Ivanhoe* performed.

PRESENTER 2

The sensational crimes of the day were also dramatised and played up and down the country to eager audiences. The most popular was *Maria Marten, or The Murder in the Red Barn*, the true story of William Corder, who murdered his mistress and buried her body in a barn. It has a gruesomeness found in few other melodramas.

PRESENTER 1

However, not all drama in the 19th century was melodrama. Apart from regular revivals of Shakespeare, there were comedies, farces, and 'serious' plays. There were also the traditional pantomimes and the brilliant comic operas of Gilbert and Sullivan.

PRESENTER 2

In the second half of the century the sensational and sentimental tone of melodrama gave way to a more subtle and realistic approach. New dramatists appeared – men like Tom Robertson, Arthur Wing Pinero and Henry Arthur Jones. Their plays dealt with the problems of class consciousness, money, marriage and sexual morality in a more mature way than the melodramas had done.

PRESENTER 1

And this was all part of a growing move in the direction of theatrical realism on the part of dramatists, actors and producers who felt that their work should be more true to life.

PRESENTER 2

They had been helped by the introduction of gas lighting to replace candles and oil-lamps. This meant that the auditorium could be

The Murder in the Red Barn

darkened during a performance and the stage lighting varied for dramatic effect.

In 1881 the first English theatre was lit entirely by electricity. From then on lighting the stage became an important theatrical skill.

PRESENTER 1

Now enter the stage designer. In the early Victorian theatre the scenery was flat and would be painted with an appropriate scene, but as stage design developed, the painted backcloth was replaced by what was called a 'box-set' – specially constructed reproductions of an actual place.

PRESENTER 2

For instance, for one play, the set consisted of a detailed reconstruction of the Central Criminal Court of the Old Bailey. The Victorian theatre went in for spectacle in a big way and their effects included train crashes, avalanches, earthquakes and gigantic stage armies. Charles Kean had no fewer than 550 in the cast of his production of *Henry V*!

PRESENTER 1

The desire to be realistic influenced costume design as well. If a play was set in the past, some effort was made to make the costumes appear authentic. However, not every management could go to the expense of historical costumes and many plays were performed in a mixture of styles.

PRESENTER 2
And who was responsible for originating, or at least sustaining, these new developments in the theatre? The answer is the famous **actor–managers** of the 19th century, who were often leading actor, play director and theatre manager all in one!

PRESENTER 1
John Philip Kemble . . . Edmund Kean . . . his son, Charles Kean . . . Samuel Phelps . . . William Charles Macready . . . just names to us now, but behind the names lies a tremendous achievement in maintaining the quality of acting and production throughout the century.

PRESENTER 2
We shall single out one of these actor–managers for closer study: William Charles Macready, thought by many to have been the greatest actor, and certainly the greatest innovator.

PRESENTER 1
He didn't want to be an actor, but went on the stage for financial reasons. He eventually became the manager of both Covent Garden and Drury Lane.

PRESENTER 2
Throughout his acting career he kept a journal in which he analysed all his performances and those of his fellow-actors. Macready wrote:
The highest reach of the player's art is to fathom the depths of the character, to trace its latent motives, to feel its finest quiverings of emotion, to comprehend the thoughts that are hidden under the words . . .

PRESENTER 1
It must have been difficult to remember these fine sentiments when he was on tour in Lincolnshire in the winter of 1834 and wrote in his journal:

MACREADY
Went to the theatre – dressed in Magistrates' room – quite convenient. When ready to go on

the stage, Mr Robertson appeared with a face full of dismay: he began to apologise, and I guessed the remainder. 'Bad house?' 'Bad? Sir, there's no one!' 'What? Nobody at all?' 'Not a soul, sir – except the Warden's party in the boxes.' 'What the d---l! Not one person in the pit or gallery?' 'Oh, yes, there are one or two.' 'Are there five?' 'Oh yes, five.' 'Then go on; we have no right to give ourselves airs if the public do not choose to come and see us; go on at once!' Mr Robertson was astonished at what he thought my philosophy, being accustomed, as he said, to be 'blown up' by his *stars* when the houses were bad. I never acted Virginius better in all my life.

PRESENTER 2
And here's what a fellow actor had to say about him:

ACTOR
I used to have walk-on parts in Mr Macready's productions – one of the mob in *Coriolanus* or a soldier in *Macbeth*. Nobody bothered about us much, so long as we got on and off at the right time. We usually didn't see the leading actors till the first night. But not with Macready. He actually used to *rehearse* the crowd scenes and the bit parts – spend a whole morning on them sometimes. And he used to act himself in rehearsals, not just tell everybody else what to do. He even bothered about our costumes. He used to get angry, of course, when the acting was bad. But the energy and the dedication of the man!

PRESENTER 1
Much of that energy and dedication was spent in restoring Shakespeare to his original text after the adulterations of the previous century. He put the Fool back in *King Lear* after nearly 200 years of the part being cut out – and he had it played by a woman!

PRESENTER 2
He retired from the stage in 1851 when still at the height of his fame. Here's how one keen London playgoer described Macready's farewell performance:

PLAYGOER
There must have been thousands outside Drury Lane theatre that night. Pouring with rain it was, an' all. And there were people crowding the

windows of the houses to get a good view. When he came we all cheered him. He'd been a favourite for nigh on 30 years, you know. He was playing Macbeth, his most famous role. When he came on the stage the audience rose to its feet, waved hats and handkerchiefs, and roared so long it was ten minutes before the play could begin. At the end, when he gave his farewell speech in front of the curtain, you could have heard a pin drop, in between the sobs of the ladies. I'll never forget Macready – and I've seen them all!

PRESENTER 1

Well, this particular playgoer may not have lived to see another actor whose fame, in the second half of the century, rivalled Macready's – Henry Irving. Irving not only achieved international fame for his genius as an actor but also gave the acting profession a much needed social boost by becoming the first theatrical knight – *Sir* Henry Irving.

PRESENTER 2

Queen Victoria, like many a monarch before

her, was an ardent theatregoer, as well as being a great admirer of Irving. She went to the theatre 800 times before the death of Prince Albert.

Irving
as Shylock

PRESENTER 1

But as her reign drew to its close, there appeared a play that might well be considered the only real classic the 19th century produced. Witty, with a farcically complicated plot and a cast of amusing English eccentrics, *The Importance of Being Earnest* by Oscar Wilde was a great success when it was first produced in 1895 and can still pull in audiences almost a century later.

PRESENTER 2

Yet brilliant though it was, it was not the kind of play to usher in a new theatrical era. That task was enthusiastically taken up by one of Wilde's fellow Irishmen, who, against strenuous opposition, was defiantly trying to turn the theatre in a totally new direction. Bernard Shaw had arrived.

ENGAGED TO BE MARRIED

An extract from *The Importance of Being Earnest* by Oscar Wilde

Lady Bracknell's nephew, ALGERNON MONCRIEFF, announces his engagement to CECILY CARDEW, the young ward of JACK WORTHING, who, in turn, has just become engaged to GWENDOLEN, Lady Bracknell's daughter. LADY BRACKNELL'S cutting remark about 'families or persons whose origin was a Terminus' refers to her discovery that Jack's parentage is unknown and that he was found as a child in a handbag in the cloakroom of Victoria railway station.

ALGERNON	I am engaged to be married to Cecily, Aunt Augusta.
LADY BRACKNELL	I beg your pardon?
CECILY	Mr Moncrieff and I are engaged to be married, Lady Bracknell.
LADY BRACKNELL	[*with a shiver, crossing to the sofa and sitting down*] I do not know whether there is anything peculiarly exciting in the air of this particular part of Hertfordshire, but the number of engagements that go on seems to me considerably above the proper average that statistics have laid down for our guidance. I think some preliminary inquiry on my part would not be out of place. Mr Worthing, is Miss Cardew at all connected with any of the larger railway stations in

47

	London? I merely desire information. Until yesterday I had no idea that were any families or persons whose origin was a Terminus. [JACK *looks perfectly furious, but restrains himself.*]
JACK	[*in a clear, cold voice*] Miss Cardew is the grand-daughter of the late Mr Thomas Cardew of 149 Belgrave Square, S.W.; Gervase Park, Dorking, Surrey; and the Sporran, Fifeshire, N.B.
LADY BRACKNELL	That sounds not unsatisfactory. Three addresses always inspire confidence, even in tradesmen. But what proof have I of their authenticity?
JACK	I have carefully preserved the Court Guides of the period. They are open to your inspection, Lady Bracknell.
LADY BRACKNELL	[*grimly*] I have known strange errors in that publication.
JACK	Miss Cardew's family solicitors are Messrs. Markby, Markby, and Markby.
LADY BRACKNELL	Markby, Markby, and Markby? A firm of the very highest position in their profession. Indeed I am told that one of the Mr Markbys is occasionally to be seen at dinner parties. So far I am satisfied.
JACK	[*very irritably*] How extremely kind of you, Lady Bracknell! I have also in my possession, you will be pleased to hear, certificates of Miss Cardew's birth, baptism, whooping cough, registration, vaccination, confirmation, and the measles; both the German and the English variety.

National Theatre production of *The Importance of Being Earnest*

LADY BRACKNELL	Ah! A life crowded with incident, I see; though perhaps somewhat too exciting for a young girl. I am not myself in favour of premature experiences! [*Rises, looks at her watch.*] Gwendolen! the time approaches for our departure. We have not a moment to lose. As a matter of form, Mr Worthing, I had better ask you if Miss Cardew has any little fortune?
JACK	Oh! about a hundred and thirty thousand pounds in the Funds. That is all. Good-bye, Lady Bracknell. So pleased to have seen you.
LADY BRACKNELL	[*sitting down again*] A moment, Mr Worthing. A hundred and thirty thousand pounds! And in the Funds! Miss Cardew seems to me a most attractive young lady, now that I look at her. Few girls of the present day have any really solid qualities, any of the qualities that last, and improve with time. We live, I regret to say, in an age of surfaces. [*To* CECILY.] Come over here, dear. [CECILY *goes across.*] Pretty child! Your dress is sadly simple, and your hair seems almost as Nature might have left it. But we can soon alter all that. A thoroughly experienced French maid produces a really marvellous result in a very brief space of time. I remember recommending one to young Lady Lancing, and after three months her own husband did not know her.
JACK	And after six months nobody knew her.
LADY BRACKNELL	[*Glares at* JACK *for a few moments. Then bends, with a practised smile to* CECILY.] Kindly turn round, sweet child. [CECILY *turns completely round.*] No, the side view is what I want. [CECILY *presents her profile.*] Yes, quite as I expected. There are distinct social possibilities in your profile. The two weak points in our age are its want of principle and its want of profile. The chin a little higher, dear. Style largely depends on the way the chin is worn. They are worn very high, just at present. Algernon!
ALGERNON	Yes, Aunt Augusta!
LADY BRACKNELL	There are distinct social possibilities in Miss Cardew's profile.
ALGERNON	Cecily is the sweetest, dearest, prettiest girl in the whole world. And I don't care twopence about social possibilities.
LADY BRACKNELL	Never speak disrespectfuly of Society, Algernon. Only people who can't get into it do that. [*To* CECILY.] Dear child, of course you know that Algernon has nothing but his debts to depend upon. But I do not approve of mercenary marriages. When I married Lord Bracknell I had no fortune of any kind. But I never dreamed for a moment of allowing that to stand in my way. Well, I suppose I must give my consent.
ALGERNON	Thank you, Aunt Augusta.
LADY BRACKNELL	Cecily, you may kiss me!
CECILY	[*kisses her*] Thank you, Lady Bracknell.
LADY BRACKNELL	You may also address me as Aunt Augusta for the future.
CECILY	Thank you, Aunt Augusta.

A WORKSHOP PERFORMANCE

Before acting the scene, study it from a director's point of view and consider some of these questions:

- How would you like to see Lady Bracknell played?
- What do you see as Jack's overriding attitude in this scene?
- What is Wilde poking fun at in the character of Lady Bracknell?
- The scene takes place in the morning-room of a manor house. How would you arrange the furniture?
- Where would you position the actors in the scene? What movements would they make?
- Gwendolen, Cecily and Algernon say very little in the scene. What would be their reactions to what *is* said?
- Are there any special points in the dialogue which you think ought to be explained to the actors?
- Where would you expect the text to make the audience laugh?
- In what other ways would you try to bring out the comedy?

TWO SKETCHES BY DICKENS

THE WEDDING DAY

THERE is to be a wedding this morning at the corner house in the terrace. The pastry-cook's people have been there half-a-dozen times already; all day yesterday there was a great stir and bustle, and they were up this morning as soon as it was light. Miss Emma Fielding is going to be married to young Mr. Harvey.

... the little housemaid is awakened from her reverie, for forth from the door of the magical corner house there runs towards her, all fluttering in smart new dress and streaming ribands, her friend Jane Adams, who comes all out of breath to redeem a solemn promise of taking her in, under cover of the confusion, to see the breakfast table spread forth in state, and — sight of sights! — her young mistress ready dressed for church.

And there, in good truth, when they have stolen up-stairs on tiptoe and edged them-selves in at the chamber-door — there is Miss Emma "looking like the sweetest pic-ter," in a white chip bonnet and orange flower, and all other elegancies becoming a bride, (with the make, shape, and quality of every article of which the girl is perfectly familiar in one moment, and never forgets to her dying day) — and there is Miss Emma's mamma in tears, and Miss Emma's papa comforting her and saying how that of course she has been long looking forward to this, and how happy she ought to be — and there too is Miss Emma's sister with her arms round her neck, and the other bridesmaid all smiles and tears, quieting the children, who would cry more but that they are so finely dressed, and yet sob for fear sister Emma should be taken away — and it is all so affecting, that the two servant-girls cry more than anybody; and Jane Adams, sitting down upon the stairs, when they have crept away, declares that her legs tremble so that she don't know what to do, and that she will say for Miss Emma, that she never had a hasty word from her, and that she does hope and pray she may be happy.

THE BASHFUL YOUNG MAN

IF the bashful young gentleman, in turning a street corner, chance to stumble suddenly upon two or three young ladies of his acquaintance, nothing can exceed his confusion and agitation. His first impulse is to make a great variety of bows, and dart past them, which he does until, observing that they wish to stop, but are uncertain whether to do so or not, he makes several feints of returning, which causes them to do the same; and at length, after a great quantity of unnecessary dodging and falling up against the other passengers, he returns and shakes hands most affectionately with all of them, in doing which he knocks out of their grasp sundry little parcels, which he hastily picks up, and returns very muddy and disordered. The chances are that the bashful young gentleman then observes it is very fine weather, and being reminded that it has only just left off raining for the first time these three days, he blushes very much, and smiles as if he had said a very good thing. The young lady who was most anxious to speak, here inquires, with an air of great commiseration, how his dear sister Harriet is to-day; to which the young gentleman, without the slightest consideration, replies with many thanks, that she is remarkably well. "Well, Mr. Hopkins!" cries the young lady, "why, we heard she was bled yesterday evening, and have been perfectly miserable about her." "Oh, ah," says the young gentleman, "so she was. Oh, she's very ill, very ill indeed." The young gentleman then shakes his head, and looks very desponding (he has been smiling perpetually up to this time), and after a short pause, gives his glove a great wrench at the wrist, and says, with a strong emphasis on the adjective, "*Good* morning, *good* morning." And making a great number of bows in acknowledgement of several little messages to his sister, walks backward a few paces, and comes with great violence against a lamp-post, knocking his hat off in the contact, which in his mental confusion and bodily pain he is going to walk away without, until a great roar from a carter attracts his attention, when he picks it up, and tries to smile cheerfully to the young ladies, who are looking back, and who, he has the satisfaction of seeing, are all laughing heartily.

ACTING IDEAS

The Wedding Day

How many scenes will you need?
How many characters – and how will you give them some individuality?
How will you bring the scene to an end?
What happens to the two servant girls?
How would you make the play into a mini-melodrama?

Take a modern wedding as the subject for an improvisation.

What stages are there on the way to the altar?
What decisions, setbacks, problems, arguments, surprises, disasters?
Who are the chief characters and how do they behave?

You might try an extended improvisation in which you link together several short scenes.
You could attempt a modern melodrama.

ACTING IDEAS

The Bashful Young Man

How would you suggest the street and the sudden meeting of the young man and the ladies?
What would the ladies be wearing and carrying?
What would they be talking about?
How would you suggest their different characters?
What new topics of conversation could you add?
(You could give the bashful young man a soliloquy to explain his feelings.)
Is there a modern equivalent of this bashful young man?
Improvise scenes in which a young person – male or female – is shy, awkward or embarrassed at an encounter with the opposite sex.

A TYPICAL VICTORIAN PLAYBILL

MARYLEBONE THEATRE,
LICENSED PURSUANT TO ACT OF PARLIAMENT.

On Monday, April 6th, 1840,
The Performance to Commence with a Drama, in Two Acts, entitled

THE RED BARN,

William Corder..Mr. Pennett,   Farmer Martin..Mr. Robotham,
George, (his Son) Miss Robotham,   Timothy Bobbin..Mr. J. Douglass,
Johnny Rawbold..Mr. Mellon,   Mr. Lee. (the Officer) Mr. Robberts,   Mr. Moor...Mr. Curling
Waiter, Mr. Lewis,   John...Mr. Cave,
Maria..Mrs. Douglass,   Dame Martin..Mrs. Robotham,   Sally..Mrs. Robberts.

SONG.   "The Charity Girl," by Master MARS.
NEAPOLITAN HORNPIPE. - **BY** - **MISS WHITE.**

After which the Laughable Farce of

MATRIMONY.

In which Mr. H. WIDDICOMB,   Mr. ATTWOOD,   and Mrs. FREWIN will appear.

A COMIC FANDANGO, BY MASTER MARS.

Mr. COLLINS, the ENGLISH PAGANINI.
Will Play a Solo on One String, Concerto, Master L.Collins, Violoncello,
Concerto. Master V. COLLINS, Violin.   Grand Concerto & Thema with Variation, (De Beriot)

The Performance to conclude with

KORAC,

Zembuca..Mr. Robberts,   Korac..Mr. Pennett,   Frederico..Miss Robotham,
Selim..Mr. Reeves,   Anselmo..Mr. Lewis,   Mirza..Mr. Douglass
Rosombiro..Mr. Robotham,   Popo..Mr. H. Widdicomb,   Ina..Mrs. Robberts,
Immalee..Mrs. Kemp,   Statia..Mrs. Robotham.

On Tuesday, Friday, and Saturday, the Performance to Commence with

ZEMBUCA.

Principal Characters by Messrs Robberts, Robotham, Douglass, Pennett, Lewis, Wilson, &c.
Mesdames Wilmot, Robberts, and Robotham.

DANCE - by - Miss WHITE.

After which the Farce of

MARRIED LIFE!!!

Characters by Messrs. Attwood, H, Widdicomb, and Mrs. Robberts.

To Conclude with the Drama, entitled

THE LAST STRUGGLE!!!

Supported by Messrs. Pennett, James, Robberts, Widdicomb, Attwood, Douglass, Lewis, &c.
Mesdames Douglass, Robberts, and Robotham.

BOXES, 2s.   PIT, 1s.   GALLERY, 6d.
NOTICE! No Bonnets admitted in the Dress Circle.
Half-price to Boxes half-past 8, to Pit a Quarter before 9 o'clock.

MORGAN, Printer 39, New Church Street adjoining the Marylebone Theatre.

Read the playbill carefully.

1 What was the schedule of performances during the week?
2 Can you show from the playbill how the management tried to produce a variety of entertainment during one evening?
3 What does the bill tell us about the proportion of actors to actresses?
4 What can you tell about *Korac* from the list of characters in it?

MARIE LLOYD (1870-1922) The Victorian era saw the rise to popularity of the Music Hall – 'theatre by the people for the people' – and Marie Lloyd was its greatest star. She moved audiences to genuine affection with her catchy songs and lively humour. (An alternative study could be the growth of the Music Hall itself.)

5 Can you think of the advantages and disadvantages of the half-price concession?
6 What is omitted from the programme that a theatregoer would need to know?
7 The word 'fandango' is hardly used now in English. Can you find out from a dictionary what it means?
8 **Farce** could be described as ridiculous or exaggerated comedy. What seems to have been a popular subject for farce in the Victorian era?
9 Why do you think no bonnets were allowed in the Dress Circle, yet seemed to be acceptable in other parts of the theatre?
10 What do you think of the design of the playbill as an advertisement?

A number of great actors have been mentioned in this unit. Choose one of them as your special study and find out what you can about their careers and their contribution to the theatre. The list of books on page 81 will help you, but you could also look up the appropriate entries in an encyclopedia. Here are some notes to get you started:

MASTER BETTY (1791-1874) The boy wonder of the age. Thousands turned out for his début at Covent Garden when he was a mere 13. A year later he played Romeo and Hamlet at Drury Lane, breaking all previous box office records. He retired when he was 17.

JOHN PHILIP KEMBLE (1757-1823) Sarah's brother. Famous for his tragic roles and was very impressive in Roman parts. Manager of Covent Garden when it was burned down and had to put up with riots from the audience when the prices were raised in the newly-built theatre.

EDMUND KEAN (1789-1833) Often considered the most brilliant actor of the period: passionate, intense, original. His performance as Sir Giles Overreach caused a woman in the audience to have hysterics and Lord Byron to have a convulsive fit. Drank heavily; career brief.

WILLIAM CHARLES MACREADY (1793-1873) The dialogue in this unit gives the outline of his career. A towering figure as both actor and manager, but found that the business side of the theatre hindered the development of his art.

SARAH SIDDONS (1755-1831) She came from the famous Kemble family of actors and was the eldest of 12. Regarded as the finest tragic actress of her day. Famous for her Lady Macbeth and Volumnia in Shakespeare's *Coriolanus*.

HENRY IRVING (1838-1905) The acting idol of the Victorian theatre. Became an actor (having changed his name from John Henry Brodribb!) at 18. By the time he was 21 he had played 428 characters on the stage. Famous for his performance in the melodrama *The Bells*.

SAMUEL PHELPS (1804-78) His great achievement was to clean up the rough-house of Sadler's Wells and raise the standard of production there. He produced 31 of Shakespeare's 34 plays in 18 years and went a long way to restoring the original texts.

JOSEPH GRIMALDI (1779-1837) The greatest clown of his day. He made pantomime sharp and satirical. Incredibly varied in his talents, his career ended tragically. His *Memoirs* were edited by Dickens. (An alternative study could be the development of pantomime in the 19th century.)

JOIN THE DISCUSSION ON . . .
MELODRAMA
Is it as good as the 'classics'?

I got the feeling from reading about melodrama that it was an inferior type of drama – not serious enough to be among the 'classics'. But it was good entertainment and audiences loved it. Isn't that what the theatre's for – to entertain people?

WELL, of course, all plays have to entertain, or at least *interest* the audience. But the great plays do more – they make you think and feel more deeply. They tell you something about life and society you didn't know before . . .

BUT it's exaggerated so much you don't believe in it . . .

MELODRAMAS say a lot about society – class divisions, exploitation by landlords, poverty, injustice – as well as portraying individual problems like alcoholism and crime. They do it all.

NOW we don't, but they did then . . .

AND the language is so false. People just didn't talk like that . . .

WELL people didn't talk like Shakespeare's characters, did they? Yet nobody suggests his dialogue is artificial . . .

THE BEHAVIOUR OF AUDIENCES
Are we too polite?

I think we're too timid today. We sit through a boring or badly acted play and nobody says a word! We even applaud at the end! I think we should protest during the performance if we think the play's not good enough. After all, we're the paying customers . . .

I don't think audiences are always polite and well behaved. Tom Courtney was acting in *Billy Liar* in the West End and there was so much disturbance in one of the circles that he stopped the play and told them if they weren't quiet he wouldn't continue. Whose fault was it that time?

DON'T be daft! You may be bored, but hundreds of others may be enjoying the play. What right have you to spoil their enjoyment?

HOW do we know? They may be too polite to object. What if you can't hear what an actor is saying? Do you shout, 'speak up!' or do you just give up?

PRESENTER 1
His first play was produced in 1892: his last was first performed in 1949 – during the first half of the 20th century drama in England was dominated by George Bernard Shaw, a gifted Irishman who came to live and work in London. After a period as novelist, music critic and drama critic, he quickly established himself as the most original and outspoken voice in the theatre.

PRESENTER 2
He was the champion of the controversial Norwegian dramatist Henrik Ibsen, who, in the last decade of the 19th century, had had ten of his plays performed to minority audiences in small London theatres.

PRESENTER 1
Ibsen was condemned by some critics . . .

PRESENTER 2
. . . one calling his play *Ghosts* 'loathsome . . . an open drain!' . . .

PRESENTER 1
. . . but applauded by others for introducing a new honesty into the drama, for facing human situations without humbug or sentimentality . . .

PRESENTER 2
. . . and for making audiences *think* about the social issues he raised. This, for a socially-conscious intellectual like Bernard Shaw, was the key to the new drama. Ibsen pricked the conscience of an audience – and Shaw set out to apply the same technique in his own plays.

PRESENTER 1
Not surprisingly, this led to a head-on clash with the Censor, who refused a licence to Shaw's first play, *Widowers' Houses*, which exposed the corruption of slum landlords.

PRESENTER 2
It was the beginning of a long battle against theatrical censorship, which was not to be won in Shaw's lifetime.

BERNARD SHAW
Did I hear you mention censorship? The Lord Chamberlain's Examiner of Plays . . . a gentleman who robs, insults and suppresses me as irresistibly as if he were the Tsar of Russia and I the meanest of his subjects. The robbery takes the form of making mc pay him

two guineas for reading every play of mine that exceeds one act in length. I do not want him to read it (at least in an official capacity: in a personal one he is welcome to). On the contrary, I strenuously resent that impertinence on his part. But I must submit in order to obtain from him an insolent and insufferable document, which I cannot read without my blood boiling, certifying that in his opinion – *his* opinion! – my play 'does not in its general tendency contain anything immoral or otherwise improper for the stage', and that the Lord Chamberlain 'allows' its performance (confound his impudence!).

PRESENTER 1

This is Shaw's unmistakable voice, which was to ring out loud and clear on almost every issue of importance in his day, both in the lengthy prefaces to his published plays and through many of his characters, for he saw the theatre as a platform for converting others to his own opinions.

BERNARD SHAW

And why not? I believe that drama can change the mind of man. Plays are meant to be a crusade for a better life. If a dramatist doesn't hold firm opinions on what a better life could be, what can he offer an audience? Charming romances?

PRESENTER 2

I ought to have known we couldn't keep Shaw out of it for very long! But, in fact, he did offer his audience more than opinions. He offered them laughter as well, for he was predominantly a writer of comedy.

PRESENTER 1

Even a play as tragic as *Saint Joan* doesn't end with the burning, but with a satirical epilogue in which Joan listens to apologies and excuses from the men who burned her.

PRESENTER 2

Shaw also managed to move the serious play out of the Victorian drawing room into the world at large. He wrote about Caesar and Cleopatra in Ancient Egypt; the early Christians in the Roman Empire; soldiers and rebels in the American War of Independence; Napoleon; Adam and Eve in the Garden of Eden; and the 'Ancients' who live in a time 'as far as thought can reach'.

PRESENTER 1

He also wrote about life and ideas in his own day: prostitution in *Mrs Warren's Profession*; religion and capitalism in *Major Barbara* (the Salvation Army heroine); socialism and evolution in *Man and Superman*; and, of course, in his most popular play, *Pygmalion*, he dealt with the topic of social class and particularly the transformation of a cockney flower girl into an apparent duchess.

PRESENTER 2

To many people, Shaw's plays are too intellectual: they are dramatised debates, rather than human stories. To his supporters, however, he is a great wit, a fountain of fine language, a stimulating thinker and a shrewd observer of character.

PRESENTER 1

He was the leading figure in what has been called the Theatre of Ideas, but, of course, there were other forms of theatre flourishing while Shaw was on his soap box, for instance, fashionable comedies by Noel Coward . . . time plays by J B Priestley . . . whimsical excursions into dream worlds by James Barrie . . . hard-hitting problem plays by John Galsworthy . . . studies of contemporary lives by Somerset Maugham . . . and attempts to revive poetic drama by T S Eliot.

PRESENTER 2

And far removed from Shaw's intellectualism, there were the plays by the Irish writers John Millington Synge and Sean O'Casey. Both comic and tragic, these expressed the struggles and follies, the dreams and disappointments of ordinary people in Dublin and the West.

PRESENTER 1

And even that leaves out many fine dramatists whose work is still being revived in theatres throughout the country.

PRESENTER 2

But the theatre is not only served by its playwrights. Many talents are needed before a play can be performed in front of an audience. During the early years of the century, a new figure appeared on the theatrical scene who would play an increasingly important role: the **producer**, or, as he is now called, the **director**.

PRESENTER 1

The old actor–managers usually produced their plays themselves, though they would have the help of the 'stage manager'.

PRESENTER 2

Without a leading figure, the actors and actresses in a company would simply work it out amongst themselves how the play should be performed.

PRESENTER 1

But increasingly there was a need for someone not involved in the actual performance to decide how the written play should be transferred onto the stage. And this is where the director came in. He became the theatrical supremo and his ascendancy was in part due to the ideas of a man named Edward Gordon Craig – the high priest of the movement that later was given the title 'Directors' Theatre'. Let's hear what Gordon Craig has to say about it:

GORDON CRAIG

You know the old proverb: a prophet is never honoured in his own country? It certainly applies to me. My ideas on the theatre were almost ignored in England, but they gained widespread support on the Continent. For that reason I chose to spend most of my life in France. Writers and actors had dominated the theatre in England for too long. Effective theatre can only be the result of one person's vision. The artist–director, the master who co-ordinates everything: costumes, lighting, design of the set, interpretation of roles and the meaning of the play. Point one.

Point two. Naturalism in design must go. I see scenic design in terms of large painted screens which are the background for the imaginative use of light . . . plus a rostrum or two that can

be moved about . . . a flight of steps, perhaps. The artist–director will suggest a location, not describe it. This allows the play to move freely from one place to another, from one time to another, without the encumbrances of the realistic set. Has it happened yet? Has the theatre seen the logic of my ideas yet? Or am I still being ignored?

PRESENTER 2

Well, both. Craig may not be a household word, but his ideas have had their influence on 20th-century theatre. We now take it for granted that a play needs a 'director' and we are no longer surprised when a stage set consists of nothing more than a backcloth, a few props and an effective use of lighting.

PRESENTER 1

So the prophet was eventually recognised in his own country. But his voice was simply one among many, each calling for its own interpretation of 'theatre' and with its own priorities.

PRESENTER 2

And in a different area to Craig, one voice that echoes even today is that of a woman named Lilian Bayliss who took over the administration of a theatre in Waterloo Road called the Royal Victoria, but popularly known as The Old Vic.

The Old Vic in 1922

PRESENTER 1

Her great mission was to provide theatre for working men and women in London. Her passion and total commitment made the Old Vic into the most renowned theatre in London, especially for the presentation of Shakespeare's plays.

PRESENTER 2

James Roose Evans, the theatre historian, describes her like this:

> She was present at almost every performance, seated in her box, its red curtains drawn across, doing her accounts, answering letters, frying sausages, ready at any moment to poke out her head to see how the audience was enjoying the play.

PRESENTER 1

And at that time (in the early part of the century) 1700 school children attended weekly matinées at the Old Vic to see Shakespeare!

PRESENTER 2

Some of our greatest actors and actresses – John Gielgud, Laurence Olivier, Ralph Richardson, Edith Evans, Peggy Ashcroft – established their reputations at the Old Vic under Lilian Bayliss. It was the standards she set that made the Old Vic the obvious choice for the establishment of a National Theatre. Of course, Shaw was a leading campaigner for a National Theatre:

BERNARD SHAW

People sometimes ask me, 'Do the English people want a National Theatre?' Of course they don't! They never wanted anything. They got the British Museum, the National Gallery, and Westminster Abbey, but they never wanted them. But once these things stood, the people were proud of them and felt the place would be incomplete without them. It will be the same with the National Theatre!

PRESENTER 1

That was in 1938. But war was to cause yet another hold-up. It wasn't till 1949 that the National Theatre Bill was passed by Parliament. In 1963 the Old Vic became the temporary home of the National Theatre while the new building went up on the South Bank – not a stone's throw from where Shakespeare's Globe Theatre had once stood.

Saint Joan – the trial scene

58

BE YOU CAPTAIN?

An extract from *Saint Joan* by George Bernard Shaw

This extract is from the opening scene of *Saint Joan*.
The setting is the castle of ROBERT DE BAUDRICOURT at Vaucouleurs.
The year is 1429.

ROBERT	Praying! Ha! You believe she prays, you idiot. I know the sort of girl that is always talking to soldiers. She shall talk to me a bit. [*He goes to the window and shouts fiercely through it*] Hallo, you there!
A GIRL'S VOICE	[*bright, strong, and rough*] Is it me, sir?
ROBERT	Yes, you.
THE VOICE	Be you captain?
ROBERT	Yes, damn your impudence, I be captain. Come up here.[*To the soldiers in the yard*] Shew her the way, you. And shove her along quick. [*He leaves the window, and returns to his place at the table, where he sits magisterially.*]
STEWARD	[*whispering*] She wants to go and be a soldier herself. She wants you to give her soldier's clothes. Armor, sir! And a sword! Actually! [*He steals behind* ROBERT.]
	[JOAN *appears in the turret doorway. She is an ablebodied country girl of 17 or 18, respectably dressed in red, with an uncommon face: eyes very wide apart and bulging as they often do in very imaginative people, a long well-shaped nose with wide nostrils, a short upper lip, resolute but full-lipped mouth, and handsome fighting chin. She comes eagerly to the table, delighted at having penetrated to Baudricourt's presence at last, and full of hope as to the result. His scowl does not check or frighten her in the least. Her voice is normally a hearty coaxing voice, very confident, very appealing, very hard to resist.*]
JOAN	[*bobbing a curtsey*] Good morning, captain squire. Captain: you are to give me a horse and armor and some soldiers, and send me to the Dauphin. Those are your orders from my Lord.
ROBERT	[*outraged*] Orders from your Lord! And who the devil may your lord be? Go back to him, and tell him that I am neither duke nor peer at his orders: I am squire of Baudricourt; and I take no orders except from the king.
JOAN	[*reassuringly*] Yes, squire: that is all right. My Lord is the King of Heaven.
ROBERT	Why, the girl's mad. [*To the* STEWARD] Why didn't you tell me so, you blockhead?
STEWARD	Sir: do not anger her: give her what she wants.
JOAN	[*impatient, but friendly*] They all say I am mad until I talk to them, squire. But you see that it is the will of God that you are to do what He has put into my mind.
ROBERT	It is the will of God that I shall send you back to your father with orders to put you under lock and key and thrash the

59

	madness out of you. What have you to say to that?
JOAN	You think you will, squire; but you will find it all coming quite different. You said you would not see me; but here I am.
STEWARD	[*appealing*] Yes, sir. You see, sir.
ROBERT	Hold your tongue, you.
STEWARD	[*abjectly*] Yes, sir.
ROBERT	[*to* JOAN *with a sour loss of confidence*] So you are presuming on my seeing you, are you?
JOAN	[*sweetly*] Yes, squire.
ROBERT	[*feeling that he has lost ground, brings down his two fists squarely on the table, and inflates his chest imposingly to cure the unwelcome and only too familiar sensation*] Now listen to me. I am going to assert myself.
JOAN	[*busily*] Please do, squire. The horse will cost sixteen francs. It is a good deal of money; but I can save it on the armor. I can find a soldier's armor that will fit me well enough; I am very hardy; and I do not need beautiful armor made to my measure like you wear. I shall not want many soldiers: the Dauphin will give me all I need to raise the siege of Orleans.
ROBERT	[*flabbergasted*] To raise the siege of Orleans!
JOAN	[*simply*] Yes, squire: that is what God is sending me to do. Three men will be enough for you to send with me if they are good men and gentle to me. They have promised to come with me. Polly and Jack and –
ROBERT	Polly!! You impudent baggage, do you dare call squire Bertrand de Poulengey Polly to my face?
JOAN	His friends call him so, squire: I did not know he had any other name. Jack –
ROBERT	That is Monsieur John of Metz, I suppose?
JOAN	Yes, squire. Jack will come willingly: he is a very kind gentleman, and gives me money to give to the poor. I think John Godsave will come, and Dick the Archer, and their servants John of Honecourt and Julian. There will be no trouble for you, squire: I have arranged it all: you have only to give the order.
ROBERT	[*contemplating her in a stupor of amazement*] Well, I am damned!
JOAN	[*with unruffled sweetness*] No, squire: God is very merciful, and the blessed saints Catherine and Margaret, who speak to me every day [*he gapes*], will intercede for you. You will go to paradise; and your name will be remembered for ever as my first helper.
ROBERT	[*to the* STEWARD, *still much bothered, but changing his tone as he pursues a new clue*] Is this true about Monsieur de Poulengey?
STEWARD	[*eagerly*] Yes, sir, and about Monsieur de Metz too. They both want to go with her.
ROBERT	[*thoughtful*] Mf! [*He goes to the window, and shouts into the courtyard.*] Hallo! You there: send Monsieur de Poulengey to me, will you? [*He turns to* JOAN.] Get out; and wait in the yard.
JOAN	[*smiling brightly at him*] Right, squire. [*She goes out.*]

60

ROBERT	[*to the* STEWARD] Go with her, you, you dithering imbecile. Stay within call; and keep your eye on her. I shall have her up here again.
STEWARD	Do so in God's name, sir. Think of those hens, the best layers in Champagne; and –
ROBERT	Think of my boot; and take your backside out of reach of it.

STUDYING A SCRIPT:
Saint Joan

These questions are directed at:

understanding the motivation of characters; finding the dramatic essentials of the scene; understanding the structure and development; studying the sub-text.

1 What contrast between Robert and Joan would you try to bring out in the opening lines of the dialogue?
2 What does Joan's line, 'Be you captain?' tell us about the way Shaw intended Joan's character to be portrayed?
3 It is unlikely that an actress playing Joan would actually match up to Shaw's description of her. Is the description therefore pointless?
4 The Squire is shocked by Joan's manner and what she demands. What is the first shock?
5 Where does Joan shock him later in the scene?
6 Give some examples from the text to illustrate the chief traits in Joan's character.
7 Quote some examples of Shaw's use of everyday, informal ('colloquial') speech from the extract. Why do you think Shaw made his characters speak in this way?
8 Why would you expect the audience to laugh at the lines:

ROBERT	Now listen to me. I am going to assert myself.

JOAN	[*busily*] Please do, squire. The horse will cost sixteen francs.

9 In what way should Robert's attitude towards Joan change during the scene?
10 Write an explanation of how you think the Steward's part ought to be played.
11 What suggestions have you for bringing out the comedy in this scene? You might consider not only points of dialogue, but also movements, facial expressions, actions and tone of voice.
12 Where would you make use of dramatic pauses; emphatic speaking; quiet speaking?
13 What is the task of a dramatist in the opening scene of a play? What would you hope to achieve in this scene?
14 Draw a sketch of a set for the scene based on the following information which Shaw supplies in the play:

The two [ROBERT *and the* STEWARD] *are in a sunny stone chamber on the first floor of the castle. At a plain strong oak table, seated in a chair to match, the captain presents his left profile. The steward stands facing him at the other side of the table, if so deprecatory a stance as his can be called standing. The mullioned 13th century window is open behind him. Near it in the corner is a turret with a narrow arched doorway leading to a winding stair which descends to the courtyard. There is a stout four-legged stool under the table and a wooden chest under the window.*

GIVE ME A FREE HAND

An extract from *Strife* by John Galsworthy

Written in 1909, John Galsworthy's play *Strife* is about the conflict between the workers in a tinplate works in Wales and the owners, who live in London. Galsworthy's compassion is shown for the plight of the men and their families as the strike drags on but his real purpose in the play is to show the damaging effects of extremism, as represented by ROBERTS, the strike leader, and ANTHONY, the chairman of the company that owns the works.

In this speech, Roberts condemns the capitalist owners and asks for the men's support to reject the terms offered for a settlement of the dispute.

ROBERTS | Mr Simon Harness is a clever man, but he has come too late. [*with intense conviction*] For all that Mr Simon Harness says, for all that Thomas, Rous, for all that any man present here can say — *We've won the fight!* [*The crowd sags nearer, looking eagerly up. With withering scorn*] You've felt the pinch o't in your bellies. You've forgotten what that fight 'as been; many times I have told you; I will tell you now this once again. The fight o' the country's body and blood against a

blood-sucker. The fight of those that spend theirselves with every blow they strike and every breath they draw, against a thing that fattens on them, and grows and grows by the law of *merciful* Nature. That thing is Capital! A thing that buys the sweat o' men's brows, and the tortures o' their brains, at its own price. *Don't I* know that? Wasn't the work o' *my* brains bought for seven hundred pounds, and hasn't one hundred thousand pounds been gained them by that seven hundred without the stirring of a finger? It is a thing that will take as much and give you as little as it can. That's *Capital!* A thing that will say – 'I'm very sorry for you, poor fellows – you have a cruel time of it, I know,' but will not give one sixpence of its dividends to help you have a better time. That's Capital! Tell me, for all their talk is there one of them that will consent to another penny on the Income Tax to help the poor? That's Capital! A white-faced, stony-hearted monster! Ye have got it on its knees; are ye to give up at the last minute to save your miserable bodies pain? When I went this morning to those old men from London, I looked into their very 'earts. One of them was sitting there – Mr Scantlebury, a mass of flesh nourished on us: sittin' there for all the world like the shareholders in this Company, that sit not moving tongue nor finger, takin' dividends – a great dumb ox that can only be roused when its food is threatened. I looked into his eyes and I saw *he was afraid* – afraid for himself and his dividends, afraid for his fees, afraid of the very shareholders he stands for; and all but one of them's afraid – like children that get into a wood at night, and start at every rustle of the leaves. I ask you, men – [*he pauses, holding out his hand till there is utter silence*] – Give me a free hand to tell them: 'Go you back to London. The men have nothing for you!' [*A murmuring.*] Give me that, an' I swear to you, within a week you shall have from London all you want.

EVANS, JAGO, AND OTHERS
A free hand! Give him a free hand! Bravo – bravo!

IMPROVISATION: SPEAKING TO THE CROWD

The theme for these improvisations is based on the speech by Roberts: one person addressing a crowd or a group of people.

The situations are suggested below. The main speaker will deliver his or her speech (Roberts' speech with its repetitions, striking imagery and rhetorical questions will help you to develop a style) and the listeners will heckle or interrupt from time to time. Either decide how the scene will end, or simply impose a time limit.

1 INDUSTRIAL DISPUTE: leader argues for coming out on strike over inadequate pay offer: some dissenting voices because of hardship and uncertainty of outcome; some strongly in favour.

2 HUSTINGS: a prospective parliamentary or local council candidate is speaking at an election meeting. He/she raises important issues in the news at present; there are questions and some heckling.

3 PRISONER-OF-WAR CAMP: there has been a theft of an important document and the prisoners are threatened with punishment if the thief doesn't own up. The prisoners protest that they know nothing about it and should not suffer for the act of an individual.

4 BOARD MEETING: there has been a drastic slump in profits and the chairman blames the managers in the various departments of the business. They claim the company offers no incentives and there is slackness at the top.

5 DRESSING ROOM OF A TEAM: the manager goes over what he/she expects from the team (who haven't been doing too well lately); the team members are not exactly happy with the way the club is being run.

6 DEPARTMENT STORE: manager/manageress speaks to some of the younger staff on their attitude to the job. It seems they are impolite, casual, inefficient and unpunctual. The assistants express their point of view.

7 HOLIDAY CAMP: the boss speaks to his/her staff on the need to be more committed to the welfare of the campers and not think of their own comforts so much. The staff resent the suggestions that they are not 100% dedicated to happy holidays for the customers.

REGIONAL ACCENTS IN DRAMA

Dialect speech can be found in every period of drama from the Middle Ages onwards, but the 20th century is remarkable for the number of regional plays it produced containing characters who spoke in dialect. Many of these plays were written for local audiences, but others were part of the mainstream of dramatic writing and were successfully produced in London.

Below are some speeches in dialect. They are intended for study and for acting – as an exercise in attempting to speak in various regional forms. Occasionally you will be helped by the spelling of a word, or by the punctuation; but for the most part you will have to supply the rhythm and intonation yourself.

To start off, try saying these sentences in as many different accents as you can:

Where are you going?

Good gracious! The plum tree's been struck by lightning!

I'm going to town tonight and I'm determined to have a good time!

Now attempt these passages in the appropriate dialect:

MIDLANDS (Nottinghamshire)

MRS PURDY

That's what I com ter tell yer. I niver knowed a word on't till a Sat'day, nor niver noticed a thing. Then she says to me, as white as a sheet, 'I've been sick every morning, Mother,' an' it com across me like a shot from a gun. I sunk down i' that chair an' couldna fetch a breath. – An' me as prided myself! I've often laughed about it, an' said I was thankful my children had all turned out so well, lads an' wenches as well, an' said it was a'cause they was all got of a Sunday – their father was too drunk a' Saturday, an' too tired o' wik-days. An' it's a fact, they've all turned out well, for I'd allers bin to chappil. Well, I've said it for a joke, but now it's turned on me. I'd better ha' kep' my tongue still.

D H LAWRENCE *The Daughter-in-Law*

IRISH

MICHAEL [to CHRISTY]

The blessing of God and the holy angels on your head, young fellow. I hear tell you're after winning all in the sports below; and wasn't it a shame I didn't bear you along with me to Kate Cassidy's wake, a fine, stout lad, the like of you, for you'd never see the match of it for flows of drink, the way when we sunk her bones at noonday in her narrow grave, there were five men, aye, and six men, stretched out retching speechless on the holy stones.

J M SYNGE *The Playboy of the Western World*

SCOTTISH

MAUSE

O hinny, hinny! Glad and proud and sorry and humbled am I, at ane and the same instant, to see my bairn ganging to testify for the truth gloriously with his mouth in council, as he did with his weapon in the field.

CUDDIE

Whisht, whisht, mither! Odds, ye daft wife, is this a time to speak o' thae things? I tell you I'll testify naething, either one way or anither. I hae spoken to Mr Poundtext, and I'll tak the Declaration, and we're to be set free if we do that.

SIR WALTER SCOTT *(Scottish extract)*

YORKSHIRE

PARKER

Do him good. No, as soon as they told me he's a southerner and his name's Gerald, I said: 'We don't want him,' I said: 'La-di-dah. That's what you're going to get from him,' I said. 'La-di-dah. What we want at Lane End — biggest chapel for miles — wi' any amount o' money in congregation — what we want is a bit o' good old Yorkshire organ-playing and choir training,' I said. 'We don't want la-di-dah.' [*With awful imitation of ultra-refined accents.*] 'Heow d'yew dew. Sow chawmed to meek your acquaintance. Eoh, dee-lateful wethah! Grr. You know what I call that stuff?

J B PRIESTLEY *When We Are Married*

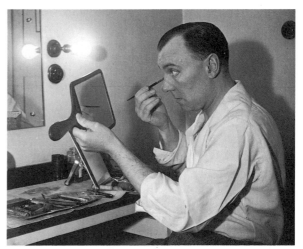

Ralph Richardson

STUDY TOPICS

The following list contains suggested topics of study for drama in the first half of the 20th century.

You will find most of the information you want in encyclopedias, and for many of the actors and dramatists mentioned, you will find biographies in a public library.

ACTORS AND ACTRESSES

Ralph Richardson   Edith Evans   Laurence Olivier

John Gielgud   Sybil Thorndike   Michael Redgrave

Study Topics

DRAMATISTS AND SOME OF THEIR PLAYS

Harley Granville Barker	*The Voysey Inheritance, Waste*
George Bernard Shaw	*Saint Joan, Man and Superman, Pygmalion, The Devil's Disciple, Arms and the Man,* etc.
Henrik Ibsen	*Ghosts, Peer Gynt, A Doll's House, The Master Builder*
John Millington Synge	*The Playboy of the Western World, Riders to the Sea*
James Barrie	*Peter Pan, The Admirable Crighton*
R C Sherriff	*Journey's End*
John Galsworthy	*Strife, Loyalties, Justice*
Somerset Maugham	*The Circle, For Services Rendered, Home and Beauty*
Harold Brighouse	*Hobson's Choice*
Sean O'Casey	*Juno and the Paycock, The Plough and the Stars*
T S Eliot	*Murder in the Cathedral, The Family Reunion*
J B Priestley	*When We Are Married, Time and the Conways*
Emlyn Williams	*The Corn is Green, Night Must Fall*
Noel Coward	*The Vortex, Hay Fever, Blithe Spirit, Private Lives*

JOIN THE DISCUSSION ON . . . DIRECTORS
Are they necessary? Do they help the actors?

If you're putting on a play, you've got to have somebody in overall charge, otherwise there'd be chaos . . .

I must say I can't bear being told how to act by a director who probably hasn't acted in his life! An actor is an artist and should be free to interpret his part as he likes.

I wouldn't like to produce a play – the responsibility! And if anything goes wrong – backstage or on stage – it's the producer – sorry, 'director' – who carries the can! I'll stick to doing costumes!

We produced *Grease* without a director. Everybody in the cast could throw in their ideas and we somehow agreed how it should be done. The actors themselves are the best producers – after all, they've got to make the play work.

I don't know. When we did *Twelfth Night* I just didn't understand some of the lines and Miss Maynard, who was directing, really helped me. In fact, she made us see the main themes in the play. She had a sort of overall view which made the play hang together.

WHAT is your experience of directors? Did they help you? Were they responsible for the success of the play? Or could you have done without them?

The author makes it clear from the start that he intends to kick us in the teeth, and go on kicking us. 'Squeamish, are you?' we can hear him saying, 'you just wait!' So he draws liberally on the vocabulary of the intestines and laces his tirades with the steamier epithets of the tripe butcher. *Punch*

The first play by an exciting new English writer burst on London last night. It is intense, angry, feverish, undisciplined. It is even crazy. But it is young, young, young. *Daily Express*

I am dismayed to learn that the 27 year old author sincerely believes his insufferable 'hero' to be representative of the younger generation. The trouble is not with the world – which was never less putrid to people in their twenties – but with a playwright who, having wit and an obvious turn for forceful writing, wastes these gifts on a character who could only be shaken into sense by being ducked in a horse pond or sentenced to a lifetime of cleaning latrines. *Evening News*

DON'T miss this play. If you are young, it will speak for you. If you are middle-aged, it will tell you what the young are feeling. *The New Statesman*

IT is the best young play of its decade. *The Observer*

PRESENTER 1

As you can see, *Look Back in Anger*, by John Osborne, received mixed reviews when it opened at the Royal Court theatre, Chelsea, in May, 1956; but it defied its hostile critics and is now considered to be a milestone in English theatrical history. What was so remarkable about it? How was it different from hundreds of other plays about young married couples quarrelling, separating and coming back together in the last act?

PRESENTER 2

Well, there are still people around who remember its impact. Bill Helmsley was a regular theatregoer in the 1950s. He might be able to put the play in perspective for us. Bill:

BILL HELMSLEY

1956 – just over ten years after the war. Everybody in this country thought great things were going to happen – a new society, more just, more compassionate, less class-dominated. But what happened? Nothing much! Business as usual! Stuck in the mire! Upper classes still had the upper hand and a writer like Somerset Maugham could call the new university students 'scum' because they were supported by the state. No, life went on with that ingrained English snobbery and complacency. To the younger generation, it was frustrating. Nothing seemed to have changed! Now what was so remarkable about *Look Back in Anger* was that its hero, Jimmy Porter, the 'working-class intellectual', expressed the frustration of his generation. He lashed out at all the cherished institutions of English society, represented in the play chiefly by Jimmy's wife, Alison, her mummy and daddy and her brother Nigel. It was exhilarating and it was funny! It made Coward, Priestley and Rattigan seem positively genteel! The audience said, 'Yes, it's true! Why hasn't anyone had the courage to say it all before?' And it opened the way for a more realistic, outspoken drama – something the theatre desperately needed to give it new life.

PRESENTER 1
Well, after that, the least we can do is to sample one of Jimmy Porter's speeches. Here he is laying into brother Nigel:

THE STRAIGHT-BACKED, CHINLESS WONDER
An extract from *Look Back in Anger* by John Osborne

JIMMY   [*moving in between them*] Have you ever seen her brother? Brother Nigel? The straight-backed, chinless wonder from Sandhurst? I only met him once myself. He asked me to step outside when I told his mother she was evil minded.

CLIFF   And did you?

JIMMY   Certainly not. He's a big chap. Well, you've never heard so many well-bred commonplaces come from beneath the same bowler hat. The Platitude from Outer Space – that's brother Nigel. He'll end up in the Cabinet one day, make no mistake. But somewhere at the back of that mind is the vague knowledge that he and his pals have been plundering and

The original Royal Court production of *Look Back in Anger*

fooling everybody for generations. [*Going upstage, and turning.*] Now Nigel is just about as vague as you can get without being actually invisible. And invisible politicians aren't much use to anyone – not even to *his* supporters! And nothing is more vague about Nigel than his knowledge. His knowledge of life and ordinary human beings is so hazy, he really deserves some sort of decoration for it – a medal inscribed 'For Vaguery in the Field'. But it wouldn't do for him to be troubled by any stabs of conscience, however vague. [*Moving down again.*] Besides, he's a patriot and an Englishman, and he doesn't like the idea that he may have been selling out his countryman all these years, so what does he do? The only thing he *can* do – seek sanctuary in his own stupidity. The only way to keep things as much like they always have been as possible, is to make any alternative too much for your poor, tiny brain to grasp. It takes some doing nowadays. It really does. But they knew all about character building at Nigel's school, and he'll make it all right. Don't you worry, he'll make it. And, what's more, he'll do it better than anybody else!

PRESENTER 2
John Osborne was the first new dramatist to be 'discovered' by The English Stage Company, which, under its director, George Devine, deliberately set out to create a Writers' Theatre. They succeeded so well that the Royal Court became the hub of theatrical London.

PRESENTER 1
The list of 'Royal Court' dramatists is an impressive one:

PRESENTER 2
John Arden, presenting sharp conflicts of principle in his plays, without taking sides, as in *Live Like Pigs*, set in a Yorkshire housing estate, and *Sergeant Musgrave's Dance*, a play that centres around three army deserters in the 1880s and poses the questions of patriotism and pacifism.

PRESENTER 1
Arnold Wesker, whose plays had a strong auto-biographical element and touched on social and political questions, as well as personal relationships. It was from Wesker's realism that the phrase 'kitchen sink' drama was coined and for a long time it was used to describe the policy of the English Stage Company.

PRESENTER 2
It wasn't quite accurate, since at least two successful dramatists at the Royal Court – N F Simpson and Ann Jellicoe – wrote in an abstract and surrealistic style. Another, Willis Hall, had a great success with his play about a British army patrol in the Malayan jungle – *The Long and the Short and the Tall*.

PRESENTER 1
What many of these plays introduced, however, was a new kind of actor with a new style of speech. The pre-war actor would almost invariably speak with a public school accent which he had acquired at a drama school. The up-and-coming actors of the sixties saw no reason to abandon their regional accents, if that's how they would normally speak. Nor did they wish to present themselves as English gentlemen from the Home Counties if they actually came from Salford or Hull. The theatre was becoming less and less the preserve of the middle class, both in the subjects of the plays and in the actors who performed them.

PRESENTER 2
And if all this was going on at the Royal Court in the heart of fashionable Chelsea, even more revolutionary theatre was being promoted in another London suburb – Stratford East. There a formidable lady with unquenchable zeal and unflagging energy had established the Theatre Workshop. She rejected the values of the West

End and created a theatre for 'the people'

PRESENTER 1

The lady's name was Joan Littlewood and, like George Devine, she set about finding new writing talent. She succeeded to such an extent that, ironically, she produced a string of successes that eventually transferred from Stratford East to the West End.

PRESENTER 2

Who were the Theatre Workshop dramatists? How did Joan Littlewood go about directing their plays? Here's Abigail McConnell, who was an actress in the Theatre Workshop company during those years:

ABIGAIL

It was hard work and great fun acting in Theatre Workshop! Joan Littlewood was a whirlwind of energy and inspiration. You were almost creating the play as you went along. You learnt your part – yes, but you had to improvise as well. The scripts were just the raw material for Joan to get to work on – for all of us to work on. I remember her saying once, 'I don't believe in the supremacy of the director, designer, actor, or even the writer. It's through collaboration that this knockabout art of the theatre survives and kicks.' And that's how she did it!

Brendan Behan gave us our breakthrough with *The Quare Fellow*, based on his years in an Irish gaol for political activities. Brendan would sit drinking in the pub opposite the theatre, throwing off bits of extra dialogue which Joan then wove into the play. Then came *The Hostage* – about a cockney soldier held as an IRA hostage in Dublin. The combination of a serious theme and a satirical approach seemed to establish the Workshop's style. Then, out of the blue came *A Taste of Honey* by Shelagh Delaney. She was only 17 when she wrote it – a really touching and funny play. Joan 'collaborated' with Shelagh on it and it became a success, not only in the West End, but on Broadway and as a film too!

After this there were what Joan called 'our Cockney improvisations' – *Fings Ain't Wot They Used T'Be* and *Sparrers Can't Sing*. I was a charlady in *Fings*. You could have knocked me down with a feather duster when they told us we were going into the West End with it!

Her last play for Theatre Workshop, some people think her best, was *Oh What a Lovely War!* Done in the form of a pierrot show on Brighton pier, it used songs and sketches to show the horrific and stupid waste of lives in the First World War. That's what she had aimed at – theatre with a punch. She was the most exciting director I've ever worked for!

PRESENTER 1

'Kitchen sink' drama . . . Theatre Workshop . . . the London theatre seemed to be moving in the direction of social realism – but not entirely.

The National Theatre

One play of a totally different kind had an enormous influence on the development of 20th-century drama. It was *Waiting for Godot*, written originally in French by Samuel Becket, an Irish dramatist living in Paris.

PRESENTER 2

It concerns two tramps, passing the time on a barren stretch of road, waiting for a mysterious character called Godot to turn up. He never does. A gross bully named Pozzo, and his slave, Lucky, appear, but not Godot. There is no plot to speak of. The dialogue is mostly comic remarks by the two tramps, yet the mood is one of desolation, unrelieved by the set which consists of a single tree on a bare stage.

PRESENTER 1

It was called 'expressionistic' theatre, because it expressed its ideas through an abstract situation, not a realistic one, and in dialogue that avoided direct explanation.

PRESENTER 2

In *Waiting for Godot* and in his later plays, Becket showed that the theatre could move in several directions at once without losing its momentum.

PRESENTER 1

He is unique, but his early plays found an echo in the work of a young dramatist named Harold Pinter who, after an early 'disaster' named *The Birthday Party* (now acknowledged to be a 'success') went on to become the major dramatist of his generation with plays like *The Caretaker, The Homecoming* and *Betrayal*.

PRESENTER 2

However, the list of 'important' dramatists in the past 20 years testifies to the vitality of the English theatre – Robert Bolt, David Storey, Joe Orton, John Mortimer, Peter Shaffer, Michael Frayn, Tom Stoppard, Alan Ayckbourn, as well as the new wave of women dramatists, like Caryl Churchill and Louise Page.

PRESENTER 1

And with the dramatists, went the directors and designers, experimenting with new techniques of production.

PRESENTER 2

Post-war theatre saw the decline of the proscenium arch stage and its replacement, especially in the newly-built theatres, by open, thrust and arena stages. These allowed more flexibility in staging and brought the actors into closer contact with the audience.

PRESENTER 1

The new National Theatre opened in 1976. It contained three theatres, each with a different type of stage: the Lyttleton, with the proscenium arch stage; the Olivier with a thrust stage; and the Cottesloe, the small experimental theatre, with an acting area that can be transformed into any shape.

PRESENTER 2

In 1982 the Barbican Centre was opened and contained two theatres which became the London base of the Royal Shakespeare Company.

PRESENTER 1

And here we need to say a word about finance, for in the 20th century there was an important shift in the way theatres were financed. Not only the 'big' companies like the National Theatre and the RSC, but also regional and small independent theatres, are now subsidised to varying extents by the government through a body called the Arts Council. This means that theatres need not depend *entirely* on the size of their audiences for their expenses.

PRESENTER 2

One such theatre group is the National Youth Theatre. For more than 20 years it has had a London season of plays acted and staffed by students from UK schools. It has given the first performance of several highly successful plays, like Peter Terson's *Zigger Zagger*.

PRESENTER 1

Even so, the majority of plays in theatres today are put on without subsidy, but with a lot of commitment and enthusiasm.

PRESENTER 2

In particular, the past two decades have seen the growth of Fringe theatre: the production of new or unfamiliar plays by groups that usually work on a shoestring. They often inject new ideas and talent into the mainstream theatre.

PRESENTER 1

With all this going on, it looks as though the theatre might even manage to survive into the 21st century!

WE'RE ON THE RUN | An extract from *Sergeant Musgrave's Dance* by John Arden

This play was first performed at the Royal Court Theatre on 22 October 1959. It is set in a mining town in the north of England 80 years ago. It is winter.

Four soldiers arrive in the town, all deserters from the army. They are led by SERGEANT MUSGRAVE, a religious idealist. He is enraged by the slaughter of innocent people in a colonial war and feels called by God to denounce the 'cruelty and greed of armies'. He comes into conflict with HURST, who has deserted, not for reasons of principle, but because he has killed an officer.

The miners in the town are in the throes of an industrial dispute and are convinced that the soldiers have been sent to break the strike.

HURST	[*breaking out suddenly*] Appropriate? Serjeant, now we've come with you so far. And every day we're in great danger. We're on the run, in red uniforms, in a black-and-white coalfield; and it's cold; and the money's running out that you stole from the Company office; and we don't know who's heard of us or how much they've heard. Isn't it time you brought out clear just what you've got in mind?
MUSGRAVE	[*ominously*] Aye? Is it? And any man else care to tell me what the time is?
ATTERCLIFFE	[*reasonably*] Now serjeant, please, easy – we're all your men, and we agreed –
HURST	All right: if we *are* your men, we've rights.
MUSGRAVE	[*savagely*] The only right *you* have is a rope around your throat and six foot six to drop from. On the run? Stolen money? I'm talking of a murdered officer, shot down in a street fight, shot down in one night's work. They put that to the rebels, but *I* know *you* were the man. We deserted, but you killed.
HURST	I'd a good reason...
MUSGRAVE	I know you had reason, else I'd not have left you alive to come with us. All I'm concerned about this minute is to tell you how you stand. And you stand in my power. But there's more to it than a bodily blackmail – isn't there? – because my power's the power of God, and that's what's brought me here and all three of you with me. You know my words and purposes – it's not just authority of the orderly room, it's not just three stripes, it's not just given to me by the reckoning of my mortal brain – well, *where* does it come from? [*He flings this question fiercely at* HURST.]
HURST	[*trying to avoid it*] All right, I'm not arguing –
MUSGRAVE	*Where!*
HURST	[*frantically defensive*] I don't believe in God!
MUSGRAVE	You don't? Then what's this! [*He jabs his thumb into* HURST'S *cheek and appears to scrape something off it.*]
HURST	Sweat.

MUSGRAVE	The coldest winter for I should think it's ten years, and the man sweats like a bird-bath!
HURST	[*driven in a moral corner*] Well, why not, because –
MUSGRAVE	[*relentless*] Go on – because?
HURST	[*browbeaten into incoherence*] All right, because I'm afraid. 'Cos I thought when I met you, I thought we'd got the same motives. To get out, get shut o' the Army – with its 'treat-you-like-dirt-but-you-do-the-dirty-work' – 'kill *him*, kill *them*, they're all bloody rebels, State of Emergency, high standard of turnout, military bearin' – so *I* thought up some killing, I said I'll get me own in. I thought o' the Rights of Man. Rights o' the Rebels: that's *me!* Then I *went.* And here's a serjeant on the road, he's took two men, he's deserted same as me, he's got money, he can bribe a civvy skipper to carry us to England… It's nowt to do wi' *God.* I don't understand all that about God, why d'you bring God into it! You've come here to tell the people and then there'd be no more war –
MUSGRAVE	[*taking him up with passionate affirmation*] Which *is* the word of God! Our message without God is a bad belch and a hiccup.

73

	You three of you, without me, are a bad belch and a hiccup. How d'you think you'd do it, if I wasn't here? Tell me, go on, tell me!
HURST	[*still in his corner*] Why then I'd – I'd – I'd tell 'em, Sarnt Musgrave, I'd bloody stand, and tell 'em, and –
MUSGRAVE	Tell 'em *what*!
HURST	[*made to appear more stupid than he really is*] All right: like, the war, the Army, colonial wars, we're treated like dirt, out there, and for to do the dirty work, and –
MUSGRAVE	[*with withering scorn*] And they'd run you in and run you up afore the clock struck five! You don't understand about God! But you think, yourself, you, alone, stupid, without a gill of discipline, illiterate, ignorant of the Scriptures – you think you can make a whole town, a whole nation, understand the cruelty and greed of armies, what it means, and how to punish it! You hadn't even took the precaution to find the cash for your travel. I paid your fare!
HURST	[*knuckling under*] All right. You paid... You're the Serjeant... All right. Tell us what to do.
MUSGRAVE	[*the tension eased*] Then we'll sit down, and we'll be easy. It's cold atween these tombs, but it's private. Sit down. Now: you can consider, and you can open your lugs and you can listen – ssh! Wait a minute...
	[*The* SLOW COLLIER *enters at one side, the* PUGNACIOUS *and* EARNEST COLLIERS *at the other. All three carry pick-hefts as clubs.*]
SLOW COLLIER	[*calls to the other two*] Four on 'em, you see. They're all here together.
PUGNACIOUS COLLIER	Setting in the graveyard, eh, like a coffin-load o' sick spooks.
EARNEST COLLIER	[*coming towards the soldiers*] Which one's the Serjeant?
MUSGRAVE	[*standing up*] Talk to me.
EARNEST COLLIER	Aye and I will too. There's a Union made at this colliery, and we're strong. When we say strike, we strike, all ends of us: that's fists, and it's pick-hefts and it's stones and it's feet. If you work in the coal-seam you carry iron on your clogs – see!
	[*He thrusts up his foot menacingly.*]
PUGNACIOUS COLLIER	And you fight for your life when it's needed.
MUSGRAVE	So do some others of us.
EARNEST COLLIER	Ah, no, lobster, *you* fight for pay. You go sailing on what they call punitive expeditions, against what you call rebels, and you shoot men down in streets. But not here. These streets is *our* streets.
MUSGRAVE	Anything else?
EARNEST COLLIER	No. Not this evening. Just so as you know, that's all.
PUGNACIOUS COLLIER	Setting in the graveyard. Look at 'em, for Godsake. Waiting for a riot and then they'll have a murder. Why don't *we* have one *now*: it's dark enough, ent it?
EARNEST COLLIER	Shut up. It'll do when it's time. Just so as they know, that's all.
	[*The* COLLIERS *turn to go.*]
MUSGRAVE	Wait a minute.
	[*They pause.*]

EARNEST COLLIER	Who told you we'd come to break the strike?
MUSGRAVE	Eh?
MUSGRAVE	Who told you?
EARNEST COLLIER	Nobody told us. We don't need to be told. You see a strike: you see soldiers: there's only one reason.
MUSGRAVE	Not this time there isn't. We haven't been sent for –
PUGNACIOUS COLLIER	Get away wi' that –
MUSGRAVE	And all soldiers aren't alike, you know. Some of us is human.
SLOW COLLIER	Arrh –
PUGNACIOUS COLLIER	[laughs]
MUSGRAVE	Now I'm in Mrs Hitchcock's bar tonight until such time as she closes it. There'll be my money on the counter, and if you want to find what I'm doing here you can come along and see. I speak fair; you take it fair. Right?
EARNEST COLLIER	No it's not right, Johnny Clever. These streets is our streets, so you learn a warning... Come on, leave 'em be, we know what they're after. Come on...

[*The* COLLIERS *go, growling threateningly.*]

A WORKSHOP PERFORMANCE

Before doing a workshop performance of the scene, consider some of these questions in discussion or in writing:

1 Subdivide the extract and explain where and in what way the dramatic mood changes from one part to the next.

2 Go through the scene as an actor or a director and study the parts of Hurst and Musgrave. What interpretation of each part would you give? What contrasts between the two characters would you bring out?

3 This is an early scene from the play and the audience has to be given certain essential information about the characters and the events leading up to the present situation. Where does Arden convey the facts? In what way does he make them dramatic?

4 The entrance of the colliers changes the dramatic emphasis. Explain the irony that arises when we, the audience, know more than the colliers do.

5 In particular, explain the irony of the Earnest Collier's speech beginning, 'Ah, no, lobster, *you* fight for pay . . .'

6 When Musgrave wipes the sweat off Hurst's cheek, there is a tense moment in the theatre (as opposed to the drama of the longer speeches). At what other points in the scene are there similar moments of dramatic tension?

7 Give some examples to show the difference in character between the Earnest Collier and the Pugnacious Collier.

8 Look carefully at the language the characters use. What decisions would you make about the way each character speaks?

9 Arden has been praised for the strong, clear, rhythmic dialogue in this play. Hurst's first speech contains a good example:

We're on the run, in red uniforms, in a black-and-white coalfield; and it's cold; and the money's running out that you stole from the Company office; and we don't know who's heard of us or how much they've heard.

Can you quote some further examples of this kind of compact, rhythmical language?

10 We know the play takes place during a cold winter. This scene is set in a churchyard. What atmosphere would you try to create on the stage and how would you do it?

ACTING TWO PINTER SKETCHES

Harold Pinter's early plays are rich in scenes of naturalistic dialogue. Characters seem to communicate with one another as much by implication and silence as in direct statements.

Here are extracts from two short plays by Pinter. You are told very little about the characters and their external situation. In pairs, decide on an interpretation of the scenes, questioning what the characters are feeling, what their social background is and why they are behaving as they are. Rehearse the scenes, with a director if you wish. Learn the dialogue and present the sketches to other members of the group.

I'M NOT HAVING HERRINGS | An extract from *Night School* by Harold Pinter

[*Two single beds. Milly is in bed. Annie enters with a tray on which is a glass of milk on a saucer, one doughnut and a plate of anchovies.*]

MILLY	I don't want the hot milk, I want it cold.
ANNIE	It is cold.
MILLY	I thought you warmed it up.
ANNIE	I did. The time I got up here, it's gone cold.
MILLY	You should have kept it in the pan. If you'd brought it up in the pan it would have still been hot.
ANNIE	I thought you said you didn't want it hot.
MILLY	I don't want it hot.
ANNIE	Well, that's what I'm saying it's cold.
MILLY	I know that. But say if I had wanted it hot. That's all I'm saying. [*She sips the milk*] It could be colder.
ANNIE	Do you want a piece of anchovy or a doughnut?
MILLY	I'll have the anchovy. What are you going to have?
ANNIE	I'm going downstairs to have a doughnut.
MILLY	You can have this one.
ANNIE	No, I've got one downstairs. You can have it after the anchovy.
MILLY	Why don't you have the anchovy?
ANNIE	You know what I wouldn't mind? I wouldn't mind a few pilchards.
MILLY	Herring. A nice bit of herring, that's what I could do with.
ANNIE	A few pilchards with a drop of vinegar. And a plate of chocolate mousse to go with it.
MILLY	Chocolate mousse?
ANNIE	Don't you remember when we had chocolate mousse at Clacton?
MILLY	Chocolate mousse wouldn't go with herrings.
ANNIE	I'm not having herrings. I'm having pilchards.

WILL WE MEET TONIGHT?

An extract from *Silence* by Harold Pinter

BATES	Will we meet tonight?
ELLEN	I don't know. *[Pause.]*
BATES	Come with me tonight.
ELLEN	Where?
BATES	Anywhere. For a walk. *[Pause.]*
ELLEN	I don't want to walk.
BATES	Why not? *[Pause.]*
ELLEN	I want to go somewhere else. *[Pause.]*
BATES	Where?
ELLEN	I don't know. *[Pause.]*
BATES	What's wrong with a walk?
ELLEN	I don't want to walk. *[Pause.]*
BATES	What do you want to do?
ELLEN	I don't know. *[Pause.]*
BATES	Do you want to go anywhere else?
ELLEN	Yes.
BATES	Where?
ELLEN	I don't know. *[Pause.]*
BATES	Do you want me to buy you a drink?
ELLEN	No. *[Pause.]*
BATES	Come for a walk.
ELLEN	No. *[Pause.]*
BATES	All right. I'll take you on a bus to the town, I know a place. My cousin runs it.
ELLEN	No. *[Silence.]*

WHICH STAGE?

Each type of stage has its advantages and drawbacks. The discussion centres on which stage you would choose for a certain play or a particular production.

Below are some notes on the four main types of stage that were reintroduced in the second half of the 20th century. When you have read them, take up some of the questions that follow to start off your discussion.

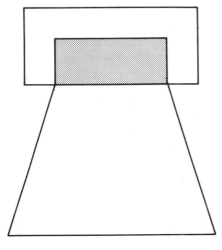

THE PROSCENIUM ARCH STAGE

The 'traditional' stage – sometimes called the 'picture-frame' stage.

The play takes place behind the 'arch'. (In the 17th century there was a platform in front on which most of the action took place. In the 18th century it was removed and turned over to the orchestral pit or to rows of seats.)

There is a sharp division between stage and audience.

The wings and backstage are useful for storing properties and scenery.

With a closed set it is possible to give a realistic depiction of a place.

The stage makes use of curtains.

The actors play to the front of the stage.

The audience faces in one direction.

THE ARENA STAGE

Sometimes called 'theatre-in-the-round'.

The stage is in the centre; the audience sits all around.

It can be 'in the round' or square – the same principle as a circus or a boxing ring.

The actors have to play to all sides. They usually make entrances and exits through the audience.

There can be no illusion created by an enclosed set as there is no back wall.

Set changes can create problems.

Great involvement by audience owing to proximity to actors.

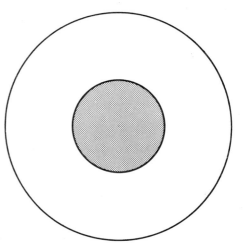

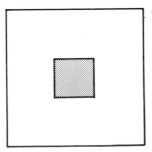

THE THRUST STAGE

This stage goes back to the Globe Theatre in Shakespeare's day.

It 'thrusts' into the audience, which sits on three sides.

There are no curtains.

All scene changes are done in full view of the audience.

The back wall can be used for scenery.

Actors have to be able to play to the three sides, not just in front.

Said to be more 'intimate' than the open or the proscenium arch stage because of the close contact between actors and audience.

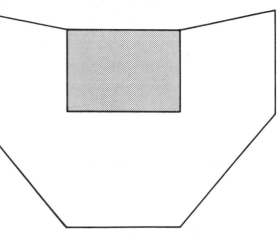

THE OPEN STAGE

Also called an 'end-stage'.

This is similar in position to the proscenium arch stage, but there is no framework.

The stage stretches across the width of the auditorium and there are no curtains.

All scene and property changes are done in full view of the audience.

Actors play to the front.

The back wall can be used for scenery.

PROMENADE PERFORMANCES

The stage may occasionally be used, but for the most part the action is presented on the floor of the theatre (the seats having been removed) and moves from one area to another.

The audience stands or sits on the floor.

POINTS TO DISCUSS

- Which stage would be best for a 'two-hander'; ie a play with only two characters?

- How would acting styles have to change according to the stage?

- You are putting on a play which consists of numerous short scenes with several changes of setting. Which stage would you choose?

- How would the lighting technique differ from one stage to another?

- As a member of the audience, which seating arrangement would you prefer?

- Do you mind seeing stagehands change the set in the theatre, or do you prefer to have the curtains closed and the scene change to take place behind them?

- Which stages give more 'freedom' to directors?

- Is a raised stage necessary at all?

79

STUDY TOPICS

1 Find out what you can about the life of a 20th-century playwright. Read at least one of his/her plays and write a critical appreciation of it. To help you, listed below are some famous dramatists with their best-known play in *italics*:

John Arden — *Sergeant Musgrave's Dance*
Alan Ayckbourn — *Bedroom Farce*
Samuel Becket — *Waiting for Godot*
Brendan Behan — *The Hostage*
Edward Bond — *Saved*
Shelagh Delaney — *A Taste of Honey*
Michael Frayn — *Noises Off*
Ann Jellicoe — *The Sport of My Mad Mother*
Joe Orton — *Loot*
John Osborne — *Look Back in Anger*
Harold Pinter — *The Caretaker*
Peter Shaffer — *The Royal Hunt of the Sun*
Tom Stoppard — *Rosencrantz and Guildenstern are Dead*

2 Write an account of a play by any 20th-century woman dramatist.

3 Write an account of the life and work of a contemporary actor or actress. If you have seen him/her acting on the stage, you could include your impressions in your study. Make good use of libraries for source material. Here are some names of performers who have a good solid body of theatrical work behind them:

Alan Bates
Tom Courtenay
Judi Dench
Albert Finney
Michael Gambon
Alan Howard
Glenda Jackson
Penelope Keith
Helen Mirren
Ian McKellen
Joan Plowright
Roger Rees
Diana Rigg
Maggie Smith
Paul Schofield

4 Write a study of a particular theatre or theatre company, such as your local theatre, The National Theatre, The Royal Shakespeare Company, The Royal Exchange in Manchester, The Crucible Theatre in Sheffield or the Glasgow Citizens' Theatre. You may have to limit your study to one aspect of the theatre but some of the following topics could be considered:

the history and development of the theatre;
the policy that governs the choice of plays;
the financial problems;
the theatre's resources (costumes, properties, scenery, etc);
how a play is chosen and the processes it goes through before it is eventually performed;
the theatre's Studio in which experimental work is done.

5 In recent years drama has been used to serve many purposes and several new types of 'theatre' have been developed. Choose one of these for your study:

Theatre in Education
Children's Theatre
Fringe or Alternative Theatre
Theatre for the Disabled
Community Theatre
Drama Festivals
Christian Theatre
Ethnic Minority Theatre
Black Theatre
Theatre Workshops
Women's Theatre
The National Youth Theatre

6 The following diagram sets out the relationship of the people who work in a theatre. As a special study, choose one (or more, if you wish) of the people in the diagram and find out as much as you can about the nature of the work they do. If you can arrange an interview with someone in your local theatre, you will get first-hand information for your study.

Theatres usually build their organisations to suit themselves, depending on the size of the theatre and the type and amount of work they do during the year: the following is a typical organisation:

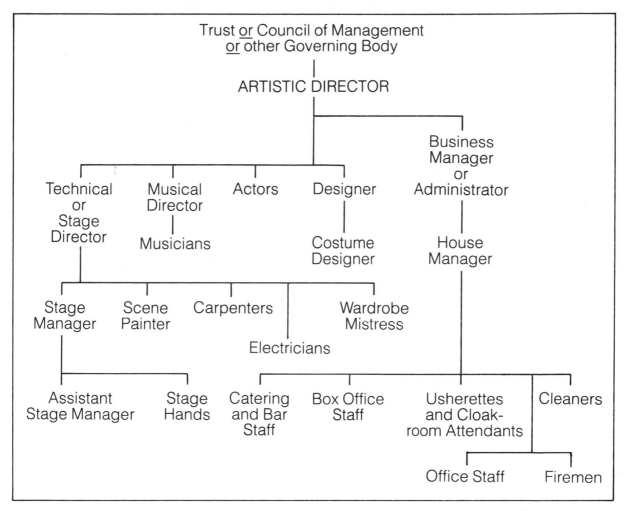

The following societies and publications could provide you with some useful information for some of the study topics.

The British Alternative Theatre Directory (John Offord Publications) for information on topics such as community theatre, performance arts, mime, children's theatre, theatre in education, festivals, etc.

The British Theatre Directory (John Offord Publications).

Who's Who in the Theatre for short biographies of leading actors, writers, directors, etc.

The Educational Drama Association, Herbert House, Cornwall Street, Birmingham 3.

The National Drama Festivals' Association, 24 Jubilee Road, Formby, Liverpool, L37 2HT.

The National Youth Theatre, 34 York Way, London, N1.

The Religious Drama Society of Great Britain, St Paul's Church, Bedford Street, London, WC2 9ED. It publishes a magazine called *Radius*.

SESAME, Christchurch, 27 Blackfriars Road, London, SE1 8NY, promotes drama for the physically and mentally handicapped.

The Young Theatre Association (the junior branch of The British Theatre Association), 9 Fitzroy Square, London W1P 6AE. It publishes regular broadsheets.

INTRODUCTORY EXERCISES

These exercises are meant to get the drama lesson going – either to bring some life to the group or to channel its natural exuberance! They can be varied and adapted to the needs of a particular group and many can be used as a lead-in to longer improvisations.

TELLING A STORY

This is a good activity to start or to end a drama session.

Everyone sits in a circle. One person begins a story – funny, serious, fantastic, it doesn't matter what kind – and must speak for half a minute. Someone is made the timekeeper and when half a minute is up, he/she calls out the name of the next person to continue the story. The last person must end the story.

WALKS

The group is asked to walk in an ordinary, relaxed way until the call is given to walk in a certain style. Here are some suggestions:

a soldier on sentry duty
along a white line, as if drunk
over thin, slippery ice
across a fast-flowing river
through deep mud, with wellingtons on
walking around a minefield

in deep thought
a 'funny' walk
over a hot desert

ONE OF THE CROWD

Everyone walks freely round the room, but their movements and attitudes change in accordance with these instructions, which are called out at intervals:
fast, but without touching or bumping
bumping and apologising
bumping and getting annoyed
ignoring one another
looking at one another
looking for someone
trying to avoid being seen
forming a bus queue
bunching to watch the Queen go by
pushing a trolley in a crowded supermarket
stop

APPLES AND PEARS

Count from 1 to 10.
Repeat the count, but instead of saying 3, say *apples* and instead of saying 7, say *pears*.
Now do it at twice the speed.

Count from 1 to 20.
Repeat the count, but this time substitute *apples* for 3 and 13 and *pears* for 7 and 17.
Do it several times, each time a little faster.
Do both exercises backwards, but *very* slowly at first.

PAIRS/PLUS

The improvisation begins with an encounter between two people and continues with the addition of more characters. It can end on a chosen climax, or simply when 'cut' is called out. Here are some suggestions to start you thinking.

PAIRS	*PLUS*
hospital visitor, patient	nurse, doctor, other patients, relatives
boss, secretary	second secretary, business colleague, the boss's boss, cleaner, tea-lady
poacher, game warden	tramp, landowner, passer-by, Animal Rights campaigner
school caretaker, student	other students, head teacher, teachers
hotel receptionist, visitor	other visitors, manager, manageress, cook

ALL KINDS OF CHAIR

Sit in a circle and place a chair in the centre.

Each person in turn starts an improvisation based upon the chair, but it must represent a different kind of chair in each improvisation, such as a deck chair, a dentist's chair, a throne, etc.

The person leading the improvisation must not say what kind of chair they have chosen: they must convey this by their acting. When the audience has guessed what the chair represents, others may join in. The scene comes to an end when the leader of the group shouts 'change'.

CONVERSATIONS

Sit in a circle.

Everyone is given a number, starting at one and going round the circle. Even numbers are told to turn their heads to the right, then to the left. Odd numbers are told to turn their heads first to the left, then to the right.

This is repeated – and each time you turn, you say 'Hello'! Now you know your neighbours.

Next, on the first turn, the even numbers start a conversation with the words: 'Good gracious! What's happened?'

Second turn, and the odd numbers begin a conversation with: 'You remind me of someone!'

When the conversations have been going for a minute or so, an appointed leader calls out 'Change!' and gives a new opening sentence.

Here are some more starting lines:
What do you think of the new teacher?
Do you feel a draught?
You don't look well. Are you all right?

POSTURES

A posture is a physical position – but we also speak of mental postures, meaning mental attitudes.

This exercise is aimed at imitating the postures of a wide range of people and studying the different parts of the body that are used to create these postures.

When you have adopted a posture, let your mind go over the various parts of the body and you will notice how each part makes its contribution to the overall effect. Ask yourself also whether there is an emotion that goes with the posture. Here are some ideas, though you may also be able to add your own:

a typist sitting at her typewriter
posing for a photograph
sitting on a chair before an interviewing board
watching an exciting moment in a horror film
sheltering from an explosion
thinking
being inspected on parade
trying on a new shoe/hat/coat
defiance
grief
shooting at a rifle range
sitting, waiting patiently
looking at yourself in a full-length mirror
throwing a javelin

SOMEONE AT THE DOOR

This simple idea can lead to a great variety of improvisations. It is based on a group of people (a family, perhaps) in a house when there is a knock at the door. Who is it? What does he (or she) want? What reactions are set up?

To start with it is useful to collect examples of people who might call at a house. They may be fairly ordinary callers, such as the milkman, the postman, the woman next door, the political canvasser or the boy scout collecting jumble. On the other hand, they may be rather unexpected – the policeman, the survivor of a crash, the sinister gentleman 'looking for someone' . . .

What attitude do you have to someone who knocks on your door? Of course, your reaction will depend on who it is, but attitudes can vary enormously, from politeness to annoyance and insult. You might introduce some of these into your work.

Try to include several characters in the sketch and give it some shape and development. If you want to push it in the direction of farce, have more than one caller coming to the house at the same time.

VOICES

The aim in this section is to study and imitate a certain kind of speaker. Note the language he or she uses; the tone of voice; the speed of delivery; the attitude to the listeners; and the accent.

Racing Commentator

And . . . they're off! And Golden Dawn is taking the lead and it looks as though he might just keep it . . . but no . . . no Happy Harry is coming up on the inside and they are neck and neck with the rest of the field already trailing . . . even the favourite Glad Tidings ridden by last year's winner Tommy Tyler . . . but it's early yet and they're coming to the first bend and it's Golden Dawn, Happy Harry, Gruesome Twosome and Flashback . . . and as they round the bend it's . . . wait . . . they're beginning to bunch and it looks as though Singapore Suzie is breaking through . . . yes and she's neck and neck with Golden Dawn . . . and . . .

Drill Sergeant

Slope arms! By the right, quick march! Left . . . right . . . left . . . right. Swing those arms! Backs straight! Heads up! Chins out! Quicken the pace! Where do you think you are – at a funeral? Put some life into it! Left . . . right . . . left . . . right. Brown, hold the rifle on your shoulder – it's not a fishing rod! Brown, do as I say! You're a soldier now, not a ballet dancer! Dress by the right! Squad, right wheel! *Right* wheel, you idiot, right! You can't wheel through a brick wall! What a shower! Now wait for it, wait for it! Squad – halt! Halt, I said! Brown, you retarded moron, see me after the parade!

Gossip

Well, yes, I just happened to be looking out of my front room window when I saw the light on in Doris's house opposite and I said to myself that's funny she and Eddie usually go down the pub on a Friday and get back late if they have a Chinese afterwards but they must have come back early I wonder why and then I saw this man pulling the curtains and there was a big smart car outside the front door and I know Doris doesn't know anybody with a car that big, nor do I for that matter, unless it was her brother back from Australia but she would have told me I'm sure I

Marcel Marceau

was only talking to her yesterday in the launderette though come to think of it she did have a lot of sheets to do and of course it wasn't my business to ask her why, you know what I'm like, so when I saw him pull the curtains I thought I'd better go across and ask if he was all right like, just in case he was a burglar, so I went over and do you know who it was? You'll never guess. Her ex-husband. The cheek!

NOW choose one of the following and first write, then deliver, a short speech, bringing out the particular style of the speaker:

a storyteller, telling a well-known story to young children

a policeman questioning a youth with a motorbike that may not be his own

a gardening expert describing and giving advice on growing vegetables

a woman demonstrating make-up in a department store

a pilot making an announcement to passengers

a clergyman giving a sermon

a sports coach talking to a team

a conspirator outlining plans

84

MIME

TWO FACES

When we perform certain tasks we often express our feelings in our facial expressions. For instance, if you are afraid of slugs and you pick one up in your fingers, you will show what you are feeling by making a grimace and looking disgusted. These mimes are based on the same idea. Perform them twice: first, with the facial expression you would naturally have; and secondly, with a completely straight face, yet feeling the emotion inside, and performing any actions that are appropriate.

cleaning out a porridge pan with your hands
carrying heavy shovelfuls of soil
pulling a splinter out of your hand
accidentally spilling boiling water over your hand
someone has put an ice cube down your back
stroking a cat
getting out of your seat in a coach and bumping
    your head on the rack

ACTIONS SPEAK LOUDER

How accurately can you mime these actions? How could the action be extended into a scene of mime?

hanging a picture   playing darts
taking a photograph   cleaning shoes
laying and lighting a camp fire   dusting
making coffee
sawing a plank of wood
buying petrol at a self-service station
putting on make-up
planting a rose bush

SHOP WINDOWS

Imagine you are a shop window dummy that can think and move, but not speak. Dress yourself and pose in the shop window.

ACTING

PRESENTER 1
An actor is given a script. He reads his part. He may even learn it. But how does he begin to develop the character he is to portray?

PRESENTER 2
Some actors study the text and analyse the psychology and motives of the character. Some leave it entirely to their intuition. Some look for parallels in their own experience. Some base their interpretation on people they have known. Some build up an imaginary life-history for their characters. Each actor will have his own technique for getting to the heart of the role he is playing.

PRESENTER 1
Without doubt, the modern approach to acting is more analytical than it was even a century ago. The preparation for getting into a part is more personal, often becoming a dialogue between the actor and the director. The text is probed, questions are asked, and alternative interpretations are tried out. It is not simply a matter of learning lines.

PRESENTER 2
This approach to acting in the 20th century has developed largely through the influence of Konstantin Stanislavski, one of the founders of the Moscow Art Theatre in 1898.

PRESENTER 1
As an actor he was appalled at his own 'mechanical' acting, that is, producing all the external mannerisms of a character, but without a corresponding feeling inside.

STANISLAVSKI
During my last tour abroad, and before in Moscow, I kept repeating mechanically those well-drilled and firmly established 'tricks' of the part – the mechanical signs of an absence of genuine feeling. In some places I tried to be as nervous and excited as possible, and for that reason performed a series of quick

STANISLAVSKI'S SYSTEM

Some of the main points of Stanislavski's system were:

1 The magic 'if'. The actor knows that the play and the setting are 'unreal', but he says to himself, how would I behave if they were real? Asking this question helps him transform the imaginary world of the play into a real one.

2 To help the magic 'if', an actor needs a strong imagination. He must ask himself questions about the part he is playing and in performance fully understand what he says and what he does.

3 An actor must concentrate his attention on what is happening on the stage and not be distracted by the 'black hole' where the audience is.

4 It is essential to relax muscular tensions, particularly in moments of strong dramatic emotion.

5 Small physical actions on the stage are very important. The actor must *believe* in them and do them as consciously as possible.

6 To bring truth and conviction to his portrayal of character, an actor should draw on his 'emotional memory', that is, the store of emotional experiences lying dormant in his subconscious mind.

7 Good communication between performers on the stage is achieved by activating the senses, particularly by listening attentively and looking directly and consciously.

8 An actor must use his intellect to understand the text of the play. He must have the will and determination to follow his part through. Also he must have enough feeling for the part to make it convincing and truthful on stage.

9 An actor does not identify with his part completely. He 'lives, weeps and laughs on the stage, and while weeping and laughing he observes his laughter and tears'.

10 'Love art in yourself, not yourself in art.'

movements; in others I tried to appear naïve and technically reproduced childishly innocent eyes; in others still I forced myself to reproduce the gait and the typical gestures of the part – the external result of a feeling that was dead. I copied naïveté, but I was not naïve; I walked with quick, short steps, but I had no feeling of an inner hurry which produced such quick steps, and so on. I exaggerated more or less skilfully, I imitated the external manifestations of feelings and actions, but at the same time I did not experience any feelings or any real need for action. As the performances went on, I acquired the mechanical habit of going through the once and for all established gymnastic exercises, which were firmly fixed as my stage habits by my muscular memory, which is so strong with actors.

PRESENTER 1

The question Stanislavski asked himself was, how can I put genuine feeling into my acting instead of relying solely on technique?

PRESENTER 2

His answer was to stress the need for physical relaxation as a preliminary to 'natural' rather than artificial acting. He also believed actors should be taught how to listen and concentrate and, above all, to believe in the parts they were playing.

STANISLAVSKI

You see, what I was aiming at was a normal living state on the stage. And in order to do it, an actor has to be physically free, in control of free muscles. His attention must be infinitely alert. He must be able to listen and observe on the stage as he would in real life, that is to say, be in contact with the person playing opposite him. He must believe in everything that is happening on the stage that is related to the play.

PRESENTER 1

Are his ideas still alive today? Do modern actors and actresses use his method, or do they work things out for themselves? Stanislavski laid great stress on relaxation, but Laurence Olivier thinks it more important to get the right poise or balance between being tense – or taut – and being relaxed.

OLIVIER

I learnt a lot about a very essential factor in acting – poise, the feeling of poise – from flying an aeroplane. It was very interesting, because your two enemies are tautness and ultra-relaxation, in anything you're trying to do, if it's cricket or any physical thing. And acting is largely a physical thing – it's to do with the senses of all sorts. It's the same equation you've got to find between tautness and over-relaxation or between under-confidence and over-confidence. It's very difficult to find just the right amount. The difficulty of acting, I've always thought, is finding the right humility towards the work and the right confidence to carry it out. With flying you have to learn at least a very exact, precise poise, between your feet being too heavy on the rudder, or your hand too heavy on the stick or too savage on the throttle.

You learn a kind of very special poise. And that I've managed to bring into the acting – frightfully useful. Or managed to remember it when I needed to. 'Now wait a minute, you're taut.' Or 'You're too relaxed'. It's come in very useful.

PRESENTER 1

What Stanislavski called 'emotional memory', delving into past experiences that lie hidden in your memory, is widely used by actors to help them understand a part. Here's Alec McCowen on how he overcame the problem of playing the Fool in *King Lear*:

ALEC McCOWEN

I found the Fool in *King Lear* a most difficult part because the lines are practically incomprehensible nowadays and because we're not quite sure what a Fool is. He's not Morecambe and Wise. There's no counterpart today. I couldn't get near the part. It was gobbledygook. Or it was until I found an 'as if', which was simply recalling myself as a small boy, when my father, who was the 'as if' for King Lear, would come home from work tired, angry, spikey, often very bad-tempered, and I used to keep him sweet; I used to amuse him, and tried to stop the row with my mother about the food being late or not what he wanted or whatever. I would cavort about and make him laugh. It's strange how vivid childhood memories are: I work from them a great deal. And once I remembered that, the part lost all its stress for me. The struggle went out of it.

PRESENTER 2

Anna Massey always works out a biography of the character she is playing in order to make the part more real for herself. Here's how she filled in the background of Miss Prism, the spinsterish governess, in *The Importance of Being Earnest*:

ANNA MASSEY

I worked out a story which made me 52. I'm too young for the part, you see. And I worked out the youngest I could be was 52. In the play there's a line, 'An injury received from the upsetting of a Gower Street omnibus', so I worked out that I went to college in Gower Street and fell in love with a German student (I was writing my novel at the time), and became a governess when I was 22. I was born in Leamington and I made Patrick Moore my father. My mother had died because I couldn't think of a mother. And because we all talk so much about Germany in the play I thought that I had spent quite a lot of time in Heidelberg, because I'd been there once; so I cast myself as a governess there.

PRESENTER 1

Stanislavski thought an actor ought to feel the emotions he was expressing, but not be completely identified with them. Here's an example from Laurence Olivier again. He was playing King Oedipus, who in the play suddenly learns that he has unknowingly killed his father and married his mother. At this point of the performance, Olivier threw back his head and uttered two great cries of anguish and terror which had a shattering effect in the theatre. It was, as one critic put it, like a 'soul torn by horror'. How did he create the effect?

OLIVIER

Most of us need secondary images to support this sort of intensity of expression. Here, in my case, all the animals that were ever caught in traps came to my aid in all sorts of variations; a favourite instance of this is the ermine who is trapped by salt being scattered upon the hard snow. This the ermine start to lick, but the cunning mixture holds fast to their tongues, keeping them prisoner though they try to tear themselves free. Trading upon this animal torment helped me to produce a horrifying enough noise. It is, as has been said, next to impossible to produce the effect of great suffering without the actor enduring some degree of it.

PRESENTER 2

Talk to any actor and he will be able to give you examples from his own experience of the approach to acting that Stanislavski pioneered, such as improvisation before working on the text, exercises in muscular relaxation, concentration, and the development of trust between the actors in a company.

PRESENTER 1

But in addition to the psychological preparation there is also the straightforward study of the play itself and a knowledge of basic stage technique. All actors have to master this as a necessity: how to use your voice; how to move on the stage; how to stand still and listen; how to enter, and how to make an exit.

EXERCISES IN THE BASIC SKILLS

Speaking THE WORDS

1 Get your tongue round these tongue-twisters!

Rubber buggy bumpers.
Which is the witch that wished the wicked wish?
Pink silk socks with shot silk spots.
Square-shaped 'saucer' scares Saskatchewan
   squaws.
I'm a critical critic critic.
I shot three shy thrushes; you shot three shy
   thrushes.
The sixth sick sheik's sixth sheep's sick.
A fat-thighed freak fries thick fish.
The three-three leaves Leith before the four-four
   for Forfar.
The horses' hard hooves hit the hard high road.

2 Putting the stress in the right place will help you
to make the meaning clear. Where would you put
the stresses in these quotations?

Ah! don't say you agree with me. When people
agree with me I always feel that I must be wrong.

I never apologise.

My aunt died of influenza: so they said . . . But it's
my belief they done the old woman in.

He maketh wars to cease unto the end of the
earth; he breaketh the bow, and cutteth the spear
in sunder. He burneth the chariot in the fire.

3 The meaning of a line will change according to
where you place the stress. How many meanings
can you put into these sentences by altering the
stress?

You said you would tell me the truth.
I told the waitress we had been waiting ages.
Where are you going?
I'm not interested in things like that!
Who said we would have supper at eight?

There are more things in heaven and earth,
   Horatio,
Than are dreamt of in your philosophy.

4 In how many ways can you say each of these
words and phrases to convey different meanings?

look yes no hello come on really
I don't know are you? first
what's the matter? quiet listen what's that?
oh hush it's dead sit down

5 A pause in a line can have a significant dramatic
effect. How many variations can you produce
in these sentences by changing the position of
the pause?

But why have you come here?

MACBETH   I have done the deed . . . Didst thou
              not hear a noise?

I don't want your thanks, or your money, or your
friendship. I simply want to be left alone.

There's no point in lying to me when you know
perfectly well I saw you steal the bracelet.

Observation

1 This is a variation of an exercise suggested by
the French actor Jean-Louis Barrault.

Take a simple object (Barrault takes a matchstick)
such as a pen, a coin, a wallet, a badge or an
envelope, and describe it in as much detail as you
can – its shape, size, colour, texture, etc. When you
have done this, describe its history: where it
originated, how it was made, who owned it . . . how
it came to be where it is now.

An alternative to this exercise is to speak in the
first person, that is, as though you were the object
itself, telling your life history and expressing all your
private thoughts and feelings about what has
happened to you up to the present time.

2 Each person in the group takes it in turn to
dress up in any kind of costume, with
accessories – the more eccentric the better. The
person enters the room, walks about briefly, then
goes out. The group have to describe in two minutes
what the person was wearing, down to the smallest
detail. The subject then returns and the accuracy of
the descriptions is checked.

3 This is similar to the previous exercise, but this
time the person entering the room does a series
of actions – opening a cupboard, sitting down,
scratching the head, looking out of the window,
slumping over a table, etc. Each action should be
brief and distinct. Mime that is clearly understood
can be used and if possible the actions should have
a dramatic continuity to them. When the person has
gone out or sat down, the group have to recount in
the correct order all the actions that have been
done.

LISTENING

1 Each person in a group of five or six states ten facts about a character they have invented. For example:

My name is Hiram Gosforth – I was born in Lithuania – my father was a reindeer farmer – I was the first of nine children – I left home when I was 16 – became a watch-maker's apprentice in Switzerland – but that got boring, so I joined a circus – as a clown – travelled all over the world – married the trapeze artist last week.

When all the characters have been presented, the group (minus one) has to recall the ten facts about each one in turn.

2 A meets B. They begin a normal conversation, but after a minute or so, they are talking at the same time about two totally different subjects and neither is listening to the other. Let this go on for a short time, then stop. Each one has to describe what the other person was talking about.

3 These scenes require four characters. The basic situation in all of them is that A overhears a conversation between B and C and reports it to D. Here are some examples (but you could add your own ideas):

A telephone conversation is tapped by someone in the Special Branch, who then reports it to the Chief.

Two characters plotting a murder are overheard by someone who reports it to the intended victim.

A young couple planning an elopement are overheard by an eavesdropper, who spills the beans to the girl's mother or father.

Two thieves planning a robbery are overheard by a 'grass' who informs the police.

The first conversation should be very detailed and the listener must report what he has heard with absolute accuracy.

WRITTEN ASSIGNMENTS

1 What different skills are needed for acting in an improvisation and in a scripted play? Quote some examples of acting in these two styles from your own experience.

2 What is it like to work as a professional actor or actress? You might try asking one of the actors at your nearest theatre for an interview. Prepare your questions beforehand and, if possible, tape-record the interview.

3 Write a 'diary' of your drama lessons for the past term. Give examples of the various kinds of work you have done, emphasising what you learnt, what you enjoyed, what difficulties you encountered and how you reacted to them.

4 Books have been written about most of our leading actors and actresses, many of whom have written autobiographies. Choose an actor or actress whose work you particularly admire and, using whatever resources are available, write (and illustrate) a study of his or her acting career.

5 Write a report on the work that went into the production of your last play. Interview the actors, the director and those who worked backstage. You might investigate such questions as: what the rehearsal schedule was; what range of acting skills was required; what problems were presented by the play; how much consideration was given to the set, the lighting, make-up and costumes; and how highly the audiences rated the production.

IMPROVISATION

Improvisations usually start with a discussion to open up the subject that has been chosen as the theme. When ideas have been generated, the improvisations can be done spontaneously or worked on to create a dramatic structure.

If the workspace is a hall or a classroom, the acting area can be defined by the group sitting in a circle, on chairs or on the floor. When an improvisation is in progress, individuals from the circle can be asked to enter the scene, sometimes with a suggestion for the character they should play and what might happen next.

When an improvisation loses pace (or gets out of hand!) the teacher can call 'cut' and go on to a new one.

Many of the improvisations suggested below can be used as the basis of a scripted play.

COMPLAINTS

This is a good theme for improvisation, since it has the drama of conflict built into it.

How do people complain? Are they always aggressive? Or do they sometimes complain in a quiet, reasonable way? How do the people complained to behave? Are they usually polite and apologetic, or fiercely resentful? When you have discussed the topic, choose a situation and work out a dramatic outline. Here are some suggestions:

a holiday camp: complaints about the food/accommodation, facilities;

a school: complaints (by students, parents, staff, people living in the neighbourhood) about discipline, behaviour, homework, the curriculum, teaching style, resources, lack of information, bullying, overwork, etc;

a shop: complaints about the quality of goods bought – such as faulty kitchen equipment, cracked crockery and garments that behave oddly in the wash; overcharging;

a television station: complaints about the weather forecasts, the content of the programmes;

space capsule: spacemen have been sadly disappointed; space is not what they were led to expect;

earth: extra-terrestrials find much to complain of on earth . . .;

a time machine: for the passengers transported to another era, not everything is quite as they expected . . .

PARENTS AND CHILDREN

Before starting the improvisation, think about the different relationships that can exist between children and parents or guardians. When do they get on well together? What causes trouble between them? On what occasions is there likely to be conflict? Are parents too strict, or do children want it too easy? Throughout the year, what are the big family occasions? When are parents most missed?

Improvise short scenes based on the following topics or statements, beginning with two or three characters and adding more as the scene develops, if you wish.

getting up in the morning: a breakfast scene
permission to come home late
an accident: who's to blame?
jobless
you're always asking for money!
our next summer holiday
hair!
unsuitable friends
who's going to do the washing-up?
to smoke, or not to smoke?
you can't go out looking like that!
motorbikes are dangerous!
school reports
when I was your age . . .
the happy birthday
the unhappy birthday
family celebration

When the scenes have been presented, discuss the way in which the relationship between parents and children was portrayed. Has your drama been 'true to life' or not?

90

BREAKING THE NEWS

A dramatic situation can be created in everyday life when bad news has to be broken to someone. The classic example is of the wife receiving a telegram to say that her husband has been killed in the war, but there are numerous other instances, the most common ones relating to births, marriages and deaths.

In developing short plays on this theme, you should first make a list of possible examples of 'news', such as:

a disappearance	the report of an accident
a pregnancy	loss of money
an engagement	something stolen
a gift	an arrest
a success or failure	

When you have chosen the news, you should build up a situation around it, with appropriate characters. You can probably make good use of the contrast between the mood of the characters before the announcement of the news and their mood after it. Try to work in other dramatic devices, such as climax, anti-climax, the use of silence and pauses, sudden outbursts of emotion, and even irony (if the audience knows what the news is before the main characters do). Finally, if you want to make the play light-hearted instead of serious, make the news good news.

ISSUES

Improvisation can be used as a means of opening up and questioning current issues. Choose one of the sentences below and build up an improvisation around it for between three and five characters. The sentence must be spoken by one of the characters at some point in the sketch.

I told you to take off that badge, didn't I?
Excuse me, but do you mind if I ask you one or two questions?
The poor get poorer and the rich get richer, don't they?
Charity? Charity begins at home!
Where are you from then?
You know we can't afford it!
You're not going – and that's final!
Brown envelope – it's probably a bill.
It's the latest fad. It'll soon pass.
We didn't do that sort of thing when I was your age.
There's something wrong with the telephone again.
Well if you won't sign, I will!
Now, about that job . . .

CHANGING THE EMOTION

People's emotions don't stay the same for very long. Happiness can easily change to sadness and gloom can become joy.

This idea can be illustrated in your improvisations. Choose an emotion and decide on a person or a group of people to express it.

Later in the scene, after the emotion has been well established, another person (or perhaps two people) must enter and change the emotion that the first set of characters are expressing. They, in turn, must resist the change as much as possible (as we do in life); but eventually the new character should win and the scene should end with the new emotion affecting everybody.

Here are some contrasting emotions which you might use:

happiness	sadness
pessimism	optimism
anger	calmness
love	hate
despair	hope

AN AMERICAN THEME

To prepare for improvisations on the theme of 'America' talk about all the American films and television programmes you have seen during the past year or so. Do any 'types' of film or programme emerge from your talk? There is certainly the 'soap', the western, the small-town family saga, the police precinct – can you think of any others? To what extent is our entertainment dominated by American culture? Is the American influence a good one or a bad one?

When you have discussed these questions, you should decide which type of American film or programme you would like to imitate. You need not satirise it, but you will probably find yourself doing so nonetheless!

Work out a plot for your play and discuss characterisation. Your aim is to convey the essential features of a type of American drama that can almost be considered part of our own cultural life.

THE INNER VOICE

Do people always say what they think? We have to admit that they don't. How can this psychological trait be demonstrated dramatically?

Choose a situation in which a character is unable or unwilling to speak his/her mind. For instance, a woman in her twenties visits her friend who has just been married. The woman meets the husband and is shown round the new house. She makes the usual conversation, saying how lovely everything is – but what she is *really* thinking is how hideous it all is!

To dramatise this, you need the following characters:

1 The newly wedded wife
2 The husband
3 The visitor as she appears to her friend (*the outer voice*)
4 The visitor as she really is: or what she is really thinking (*the inner voice*)

3 and 4 are, therefore, the same person, but are played by two people. After the visitor has spoken, the inner voice says what she is actually thinking.

VISITOR	It's lovely to see you again, darling!
INNER VOICE	The back of beyond! I'm not doing that drive again!
VISITOR	And your curtains! They're lovely! Beautiful!
INNER VOICE	Aren't they awful! She never did have any taste!

The two voices go on throughout the sketch. It might be an effective way of ending the sketch if the inner voice suddenly became the outer voice and the visitor said just what she thought!

Think of some other situations where you can have a character, or characters with an 'inner voice'.

YOUTH AND AGE

Before starting this improvisation, discuss the theme in the group. Do people remain the same throughout their lives, or do they change? We know we change physically, but do we change in our attitudes, beliefs and ideas also?

If you decide that some people *do* change, then you can illustrate this in a dramatic way by developing two scenes: the first showing the character in youth (with one set of beliefs); the second showing him or her in later life when the beliefs have changed. For instance, a failure can become a success, a racist can become tolerant, the person determined never to marry becomes a husband or wife.

You will have to decide on the particular situation, choose additional characters (who can be the same in both scenes) and, if necessary, have a narrator linking the two scenes together. In the second scene, try to explain in the dialogue why or how the change has taken place. Here are some suggestions:

Scene 1 : THEN	Scene 2 : NOW
1 boy or girl from a very poor family – suffering from hardship – determined to get on in the world	the successful man/women – how have they become successful? – what attitude do they now have to poor people?
2 a person who is very left-wing (Communist) or very right-wing (Tory or Fascist) – his/her ideas about society – what should be done?	the character has changed his/her ideas completely – why? – what caused the change? – someone from the past enters to remind him/her of what he/she was
3 young people in love – decide to get married – their hopes of a long, happy relationship – children – home	what actually happened?
4 successful young sportsman – praise from family and friends – determination to become professional – go places	was he/she successful? – what job did he/she eventually take? – does he/she live on past glories? – what do friends say now?

Variation

It can be dramatically effective to reverse the scenes. For instance, playing Scene 2 before Scene 1 can make the sketch very ironical because we, the audience, know what will happen in the future, but the characters do not.

MAKE-UP

Before starting to make-up a face, either your own or someone else's, remember these two principles:
– Use the natural features as much as possible.
– Don't overdo it! Too much make-up looks artificial and amateurish.
Here are some other make-up tips:

EYES: If you want to emphasise the eyes, highlight the upper and the lower lids. If the eyes have to appear sunken, darken the eyelids and underbrows.
To make the eyes appear larger, apply a fine dark line to the edges of the upper and lower lids, then make the lines meet beyond the corner of the eye.

EYEBROWS: Eyebrows can be rubbed flat with moistened soap and covered with foundation. They can then be painted over in any shape you wish.

MOUTH: Foundation can obliterate the lips and by outlining and filling in with carmine, almost any pair of lips can be suggested.
Drooping corners suggest depression. Rising corners and a broad upper lip suggest cheerfulness. A straight mouth makes a character look severe. Full lips suggest sensuousness.

NOSE: Heavy shading on either side will make the nose seem narrower. Highlighting on the ridge in addition to the shading will make it appear long and straight.

MOUSTACHES AND BEARDS: Use crepe hair and stick it in place with spirit gum, but draw the outline of the moustache or beard first. For beards, work upwards from the chin so that the tufts of hair overlap, then trim with scissors.

MAKING-UP 1 : STRAIGHT

A 'straight role' is one in which an actor need not change his ordinary appearance, and the make-up required is minimal and basic. Here's how a young actor in a straight part would be made up:

Cleaning: Use a cleansing cream and wipe the face dry.

Foundation: Use a combination of light ivory and brownish brick red – that is, 5 and 9, the standard foundation. Paint stripes on the forehead, cheeks and chin and blend them in.

Shading: Put a slight shadow on either side of the nose and under the cheekbone, using a combination of brown (16) and crimson lake (25).

Highlights: Light ivory (5) on the cheekbones.

Colouring: For cheeks use 9 (brownish brick red), fading into carmine.

For lips, use 9 very lightly, then outline them with a trace of crimson lake.

For the eyes, add a touch of 9 to the eye-hollow. On the eyelids, use a dull, darkish brown (16) and crimson lake. Put a line along the lashes with an eyebrow pencil. Use the same pencil to shape the eyebrows.

Powder: Use a rose or brownish blending powder to set the make-up.

93

MAKING-UP 2 : AN OLDER WOMAN

In general, the foundation is more sallow than for the straight make-up. The shadows are deeper and the highlights more pronounced (making eyes more sunken and cheekbones more prominent). Lips are thinner and paler. The natural lines of the face are accentuated. There may be pouches under the eyes and greying hair.

Foundation: For a sallow appearance, use 6. Add light rose (2½) for a healthier tone or brick red (9) for an outdoor complexion.

Shading: Use deep brown (16) mixed with crimson lake (25) or crimson lake mixed with light grey (31).
Areas to shade: furrows on brow and cheeks; temples; inner corner of eye-hollow; pouches under the eyes; under cheek-bones; folds in chin and neck.

Hair: Use white or light grey hair powder. Streak with white greasepaint (20).

Powder: Use rose or neutral blending powder.

Apply liquid make-up to neck, arms and hands.

Highlights: Use light ivory or white. Highlights should be put above shaded lines and furrows and horizontally in the centre of the pouches under the eyes. The outer part of the eye-hollow should be high-lighted to give a drooping effect when the inside is shaded.

Colouring: Carmine 2 or 3, lightly applied on cheeks. For lining lips use carmine 3. For lining eyes use mauve shades of eye-shadow. Put a line along the lashes with dark grey (32) or crim-son lake (25).
To give a tired effect apply white (20) or light grey (31) to the eyebrows.

MAKE-UP EXERCISES

1 Choose a person to be made-up and decide whether he or she is to play a straight or a character part. Take it in turn to apply the foundation, shading, colouring, lining and powder. Discuss the processes and the results.

2 Without applying a foundation, experiment with liners in pairs or small groups. Try to create contrasting effects of age and character, particularly with the eyes.

3 Choose a character from a play you have read recently and make up one of the group for the part.

4 Draw the outline of a face and using the information in this section, describe in writing how you would make up a character of your own choosing.

5 Draw some moustaches and suggest the types of character who might wear them – both modern and period.

STAGE DESIGN

PRESENTER 1

The expression 'stage-set' is comparatively recent in the history of the theatre. It means the scenery or any construction on the stage that represents where the action of the play takes place.

PRESENTER 2

In the Greek and the Elizabethan theatres, the permanent stage itself was the set and could be used to represent various locations. The guildsmen of the Middle Ages came nearer to creating stage-sets when they built the scenery for their pageants, though on a very small scale.

PRESENTER 1

Set design as we now understand it really began in Italy in the 17th and 18th centuries. The laws of perspective were discovered and artists produced magnificent architectural paintings as the backdrop to plays.

PRESENTER 2

In England, when the Restoration theatres replaced the Elizabethan ones, the proscenium arch was introduced and scenery was used at the back of the stage and in the side wings.

PRESENTER 1

In the mid 18th century David Garrick brought an artist from Alsace named de Loutherbourg to Drury Lane. His set designs were based on natural landscapes and he produced wonderful atmospheric effects, such as moonlight and storms.

PRESENTER 2

Loutherbourg was followed by William Capon, who introduced an historical accuracy into his designs and gave plays a more realistic background. By the middle of the 19th century, however, scene design had lost its originality and standard sets, such as a grove, a temple, a palace, were used without attempting to suggest the particular place that the play demanded.

PRESENTER 1

Then came box sets – 3-dimensional replicas of actual places, like drawing rooms and courts of law. Electric lighting added to the realistic effect.

PRESENTER 2

In 1896 the first revolving stage was used in England, bringing greater flexibility to the stage-set.

PRESENTER 1

Then a reaction (if you'll excuse the pun!) set in against realism, led by an artist named Gordon Craig, who produced designs that were abstract and symbolical. He used dramatic lighting effects and rejected naturalistic detail as being trivial and unnecessary.

PRESENTER 2

But in spite of Craig's theories, many set-designers continued in the traditional style and painted scenery or built realistic sets. The two forms existed side-by-side.

PRESENTER 1

In today's theatre, audiences are prepared for any type of set. Technical expertise in large theatres can create vast, ingenious sets that change before your very eyes. Some sets are simple constructions representing the theme of the play only; others are boxed in and realistic to the smallest picture on the wall. Occasionally a play is performed without a set. There is simply a bare stage and a few props.

STUDY TOPICS

1 Can you give some examples of stage-sets you have seen in the theatre? How effective were they? How did they differ from one another? How much did they contribute to the effectiveness of the play?

2 You will probably find at least one book on stage-design in your local library. You could copy some of the illustrations and write an accompanying commentary to show the wide range of stage-sets used in the modern theatre.

3 Write an account of the life and ideas of Gordon Craig and illustrate it with some reproductions of his stage designs.

4 Actually the best thing that could happen to our theatre at this very moment would be for playwrights and actors and directors to be handed a bare stage on which no scenery could be placed, and then be told that they must write and act and direct for this stage. In no time we should have the most exciting theatre in the world.

ROBERT EDMOND JONES *Towards a New Stage*

What is the reasoning behind this statement? Do you agree or disagree with it?

DESIGNING A SET

In pairs or small groups, discuss set designs for the following plays and try to come up with some preliminary drawings. Compare your efforts and decide which is the most effective.

1 *Waiting for Godot*

Becket's description of the scene is this:

ACT 1   *A country road. A tree. Evening.*
ACT 2   *Next day. Same time. Same place.*

2 *Macbeth*

The scenes are as follows:

A camp

A barren heath
The palace at Forres
Inverness: Macbeth's castle
A court in Macbeth's castle
Before Macbeth's castle
The hall of the palace at Forres [banquet scene]
Lennox's castle in Scotland
A cavern
England: before the palace of King Edward
Dunsinane: a room in the castle
The country near Dunsinane
Dunsinane: a court in the castle
Country near Birnam
Dunsinane: before the castle gate
Dunsinane: within the castle

3 *Spring and Port Wine*

The living room, kitchen and scullery of the Crompton home. Early Friday evening.
Most of the stage is taken up by the living room, which has a bay window down right, a door to the hall up centre and one to the kitchen up left. The kitchen also has a door in its downstage wall which leads to the scullery. The scullery extends down left of the living-room wall and in its own left wall is the back door of the house. The front door is off up right of the corridor centre. The house is a comfortable, prosperous, working-class home. The furniture is fairly modern, everything is polished and well cared for. There is nothing cheap or vulgar.

Waiting for Godot